The Department of Defense Posture for Artificial Intelligence

Assessment and Recommendations

DANIELLE C. TARRAF, WILLIAM SHELTON, EDWARD PARKER, BRIEN ALKIRE,
DIANA GEHLHAUS CAREW, JUSTIN GRANA, ALEXIS LEVEDAHL, JASMIN LÉVEILLÉ,
JARED MONDSCHEIN, JAMES RYSEFF, ALI WYNE, DAN ELINOFF, EDWARD GEIST,
BENJAMIN N. HARRIS, ERIC HUI, CEDRIC KENNEY, SYDNE NEWBERRY,
CHANDLER SACHS, PETER SCHIRMER, DANIELLE SCHLANG, VICTORIA SMITH,
ABBIE TINGSTAD, PADMAJA VEDULA, KRISTIN WARREN

December 2019
Prepared for the Office of the Secretary of Defense
Approved for public release; distribution unlimited

NATIONAL DEFENSE RESEARCH INSTITUTE

For more information on this publication, visit www.rand.org/t/RR4229

Library of Congress Cataloging-in-Publication Data is available for this publication.
ISBN: 978-1-9774-0405-3

Published by the RAND Corporation, Santa Monica, Calif.
© Copyright 2019 RAND Corporation
RAND® is a registered trademark.

Support RAND
Make a tax-deductible charitable contribution at
www.rand.org/giving/contribute

www.rand.org

Preface

Section 238(e) of the National Defense Authorization Act of fiscal year 2019 directed the senior official within the Department of Defense (DoD) with principal responsibility for coordinating artificial intelligence (AI) activities for DoD to complete a study on AI topics. In December 2018, the director of the DoD Joint Artificial Intelligence Center (JAIC) asked the National Defense Research Institute (NDRI) at the RAND Corporation to conduct an independent assessment of DoD's posture in AI in the spirit of the study on AI topics legislated in Section 238(e).

After consultation with the congressional staffers responsible for drafting the legislation, the RAND NDRI team distilled the congressional language into three key objectives for the study: (1) to assess the state of AI relevant to DoD and address misconceptions; (2) to carry out an independent introspective assessment of the posture of DoD in AI; and (3) to develop recommendations for internal actions, external engagements, and legislative actions to improve DoD's posture in AI. In keeping with the language of the legislation, the RAND NDRI team collected insights into these three questions through semistructured interviews with experts within DoD, other federal agencies, academia, relevant advisory committees, and the commercial sector. The team augmented this broad input with an independent review of the portfolio of DoD investments in AI, a set of historical case studies, reviews of relevant literature, and the technical and other expertise resident in the team to arrive at the findings and recommendations presented in this report and associated annex, aligned with the three key objectives of Section 238(e) as distilled above.

This study should be of interest to DoD leaders and stakeholders in AI and to congressional audiences with an interest in AI. The research was sponsored by the DoD JAIC and was conducted within the Acquisition and Technology Policy Center of the RAND National Defense Research Institute, a federally funded research and development center sponsored by the Office of the Secretary of Defense, the Joint Staff, the Unified Combatant Commands, the Navy, the Marine Corps, the defense agencies, and the defense Intelligence Community.

For more information on the RAND Acquisition and Technology Policy Center, see www.rand.org/nsrd/ndri/centers/atp or contact the director (contact information is provided on the webpage).

Contents

Boxes, Figures, and Tables

Boxes

Figures

Tables

Summary

Context

Section 238(e) of the fiscal year (FY) 2019 National Defense Authorization Act (NDAA) mandated that the senior Department of Defense (DoD) official with principal responsibility for the coordination of DoD's efforts to develop, mature, and transition artificial intelligence (AI) technologies into operational use carry out a study on AI topics. In December 2018, Lieutenant General John N. T. "Jack" Shanahan, director of the Joint Artificial Intelligence Center (JAIC), asked the RAND Corporation's National Defense Research Institute (NDRI) to conduct a study to independently assess DoD's posture in AI in the spirit of Section 238(e). After consultation with the congressional staffers responsible for drafting the legislation, we distilled the congressional language to the following three objectives for this study:

1. Assess the state of AI relevant to DoD and address misconceptions.
2. Carry out an independent introspective assessment of DoD's posture for AI.
3. Develop a set of recommendations for internal DoD actions, external engagements, and potential legislative or regulatory actions to enhance DoD's posture in AI.

Approach

The starting point of our study was the underlying premise, implicit in the language of Section 238 of the FY 2019 NDAA, that DoD needs to be competitively positioned for AI. Motivated in part by the desire to remain agnostic about the precise definition of AI, we posed the question: How well is DoD positioned to build or acquire, test, transition, and sustain—at scale—a set of technologies falling under the broad AI umbrella?

We distilled the information needed to answer that question into six dimensions that form the analytical framework for our posture assessment. These are *organization* (executive-level view of DoD, including vision, strategy, organizational structures, and resources committed); *advancement* (research, development, prototyping, and verification, validation, testing, and evaluation of the technology); *adoption* (technology procurement, fielding, and life-cycle management and redesign of concepts and processes to make best use of the technologies); *innovation* (internal culture for innovation and mechanisms for bringing in external innovations or innovators); *data* (data as a resource, data governance, and supporting infrastructure allowing the leveraging of data); and *talent* (DoD needs and mechanisms for cultivating and growing talent).

We initiated four parallel data collection and analysis efforts. The first line of effort collected input from 59 DoD interviews and nine other federal government interviews relating to all six dimensions of posture assessment to help us better understand the current DoD and federal landscape. The second line of effort collected input from 25 industry interviews and nine academic interviews relating to all six dimensions of posture assessment to help us better understand best practices and lessons learned. The third line of effort developed six historical case studies to help us understand lessons learned from history that might be extrapolated to the current posture assessment. The data and insights from these three lines of effort were synthesized and supplemented by two additional sources: first, the team's technical and other expertise, and second, our consultation of the literature. Emerging themes and evidence across these multiple sources were then used as the basis for our assessments of the state of AI and DoD's posture in AI, and to develop a set of recommendations.[1]

The fourth effort was a quantitative assessment of DoD's current investment portfolio in AI; that effort is discussed in an annex to this report that is not publicly available.

Assessment

DoD-Relevant State of AI

The interplay of three elements ultimately affects DoD's success in scaling AI in support of its mission.[2] These elements are (1) the *technologies and capabilities space*, (2) the *spectrum of DoD AI applications*, and (3) the *investment space and time horizon*. It is important for decisionmakers to understand each of these elements and, more significantly, how these elements interrelate.

In particular, DoD AI applications fall along a spectrum characterized by four independent factors: operating environment, resources, tempo, and implications of failure. Where an application falls on this spectrum has important implications for the choice and feasibility of AI solutions and their expected timeline for availability. Although this characterization of the spectrum might not be intuitive for decisionmakers, it can be reasonably mapped to something that is easily understood—specifically, three broad categories of AI applications: enterprise AI, mission-support AI, and operational AI. With this characterization in mind, the salient points of our assessment of the state of AI are as follows.

What are prominent recent advancements in the technologies and capabilities space? Many different technologies underpin AI. One area

---

[1]   The government interviews were conducted between April 3, 2019, and August 29, 2019. We have no reason to believe that the emergent themes, findings, and recommendations regarding the DoD posture for AI are affected by DoD activity in the intervening period. However, the status of certain DoD initiatives might have evolved since interviews were conducted, in ways that are not reflected in this report.

[2]   By *scaling AI*, we mean moving beyond technology demonstrations, prototypes, pilots, and isolated uses to deployment of AI to its full potential across DoD.

of significant recent technological advances is in supervised machine learning, particularly deep learning, leading to notable progress in classification and prediction tasks as demonstrated by breakthroughs in image, text, and speech problems. Another set of publicly lauded advances is in deep reinforcement learning, with progress shown in strategy games and computer games, though the real-world implications of these advances remain unclear. All these advances are predicated on the availability of large labeled data sets and significant computing power to train the algorithms.

How might these recent AI developments enhance DoD's mission, and what would it take to scale them across DoD applications? From a technical standpoint, enterprise AI currently presents low-hanging fruit for DoD, while mission-support AI and, especially, operational AI remain further out on the horizon for several reasons: the fragility and lack of robustness of these algorithms, those algorithms being optimized for commercial rather than DoD uses, and their artisanal nature. Nonetheless, scaling enterprise AI will not be an easy task. Indeed, it will require careful strategy and execution coupled with significant investments in infrastructure and enablers.

What does that mean for DoD? DoD should pursue opportunities to leverage new advances across enterprise AI, mission-support AI, and operational AI—with particular attention paid to verification, validation, testing, and evaluation (VVT&E), especially to the latter two categories of applications. However, it is important for DoD to maintain realistic expectations for both performance and timelines in going from demonstrations of the art of the possible to deployments at scale. As a rule of thumb, investments made starting today can be expected to yield at-scale deployment in the near term for enterprise AI, in the middle term for most mission-support AI, and in the long term for most operational AI. Furthermore, sustained, accompanying investments in infrastructure and enablers and VVT&E are needed to ensure success.

DoD Posture in AI

Although we see some positive signs, our assessment is that DoD's posture in AI is significantly challenged across all dimensions of our assessment. We highlight the most critical points here.

- *Organization:* DoD articulated an ambitious vision for DoD AI, developed a far-reaching AI strategy, and stood up the JAIC as the focal point of AI within DoD, with the mandate to scale AI and its impact throughout DoD. However,
    - DoD AI strategy lacks baselines and metrics to meaningfully assess progress toward its vision.
    - DoD failed to provide the JAIC with visibility, authorities, and resource commitments, making it exceedingly difficult for the JAIC to succeed in its assigned mandate.
- *Organization:* Several of the armed services developed AI strategy annexes to complement DoD's AI strategy. As with DoD's AI strategy, the service annexes generally lack baselines and metrics to meaningfully assess progress. Moreover, although the services have created centralized AI organizations, the roles, mandates, and authorities of these organizations within the services remain unclear.
- *Advancement and adoption:* The current state of AI VVT&E is nowhere close to ensuring the performance and safety of AI applications, particularly where safety-critical systems are concerned. Although this is not a uniquely DoD problem, it is one that significantly affects DoD.
- *Data:* DoD faces multiple challenges in data, including the lack of data. When data do exist, impediments to their use include lack of traceability, understandability, access, and interoperability of data collected by different systems.
- *Talent:* DoD lacks clear mechanisms for growing, tracking, and cultivating AI talent, even as it faces a very tight AI job market.

Recommendations

We offer 11 recommendations for addressing the most-critical challenges. Strategic recommendations are marked "S," and tactical ones are marked "T."

Our first strategic recommendation addresses DoD's vision for AI and the governance structures that would support this vision as articulated in the DoD AI strategy.

Recommendation S-1: DoD should adapt AI governance structures that align authorities and resources with their mission of scaling AI.

Based on the insights from our study, notably the need for centralized efforts supported at the highest levels to enact transformation and scale AI, we propose two specific options for consideration by DoD in Chapter Five. The first option would likely require congressional support to execute; the second could be executed without such support because it aligns with current DoD procedures and organizational structures.

Regardless of how DoD incorporates Recommendation S-1, Recommendations T-1, T-3, and T-4 outline the steps that the JAIC needs to take to have a better chance of succeeding at its mission, and Recommendation T-2 outlines the steps that the centralized service AI organizations similarly need to take to have a better chance of succeeding at their respective missions.

Recommendation T-1: The JAIC should develop a five-year strategic road map—backed by baselines and metrics, and expected to be the first of several to follow—to execute the mission of scaling AI and its impact.

Recommendation T-2: Each of the centralized AI service organizations should develop a five-year strategic road map, backed by baselines and metrics, to execute its mandate.

Recommendation T-3: The JAIC, working in partnership with the Under Secretary of Defense (USD) for Research and Engineering (R&E), the USD for Acquisition and Sustainment (A&S), the Chairman of the Joint Chiefs of Staff, and the service AI representatives on the JAIC council, should carry out annual or biannual portfolio reviews of DoD-wide investments in AI.

Recommendation T-4: The JAIC should organize a technical workshop, annually or biannually, showcasing AI programs DoD-wide.

Our next strategic recommendation and the accompanying tactical one address the critical question of VVT&E.

Recommendation S-2: DoD should advance the science and practice of VVT&E of AI systems, working in close partnership with industry and academia. The JAIC, working closely with the USDE (R&E), the USD(A&S), and the Office of Operational Test and Evaluation, should take the lead in coordinating this effort, both internally and with external partners.

Recommendation T-5: All funded AI efforts should include a budget for AI VVT&E, including any critically needed testing infrastructure.

Our next recommendation is a tactical one that that speaks to the need to bring developers, users, and operators of AI technologies together to enhance success.

Recommendation T-6: All agencies within DoD should create or strengthen mechanisms for connecting AI researchers, technology developers, and operators.

Our third strategic recommendation, and the accompanying tactical recommendation, address data as critical resources for DoD, the need for a transformation in the overall culture of DoD to best leverage data, and potential avenues for enhancing innovation.

Recommendation S-3: DoD should recognize data as critical resources, continue instituting practices for their collection and curation, and increase sharing while resolving issues in protecting the data after sharing and during analysis and use.

Recommendation T-7: The chief data officer should make a selection of DoD data sets available to the AI community to spur innovation and enhance external engagement with DoD.

Our final strategic recommendation addresses the critical question of talent and points to a cultural shift that needs to occur to better enable DoD to access the AI talent pool.

Recommendation S-4: DoD should embrace permeability, and an appropriate level of openness, as a means of enhancing DoD's access to AI talent.

Acknowledgments

We thank Lt Gen John N.T. "Jack" Shanahan, director of the Joint Artificial Intelligence Center, Office of the Department of Defense Chief Information Officer, for entrusting us with this study. We thank Mark Beall, director of strategic engagement and policy, Joint Artificial Intelligence Center, for his support of our study in his role as action officer.

We thank Wilton Virgo and Andrew Kelley, Office of Cost Assessment and Program Evaluation, for making the raw data on Department of Defense–wide artificial intelligence investments from their President's Budget 2019 and 2020 data calls available to us for the portfolio review. We thank Corbin Evans and Shane Shaneman of the National Defense Industrial Association for the introductions they provided.

Our study benefited from the enthusiastic support and generous participation of numerous individuals in the Department of Defense, other federal government organizations and agencies, industry, and academia. Because of our study's rules of engagement, we will not identify the individuals we interviewed here. We emphasize that their inputs and perspectives were critical to our study, and we greatly appreciate their time and engagement.

Several RAND Corporation colleagues offered their help and support along the way. We thank RAND Project AIR FORCE leadership, particularly Ted Harshberger, Obaid Younossi, and James Chow, for providing introductions to Air Force stakeholders. We thank RAND Arroyo Center leadership, particularly Sally Sleeper and Bruce Held, for supporting our team's outreach to Army stakeholders. We thank the

RAND National Security Research Division (NSRD) leadership, particularly Laura Baldwin, John Winkler, and Paul DeLuca, for connecting us with interviewees within its sponsor base in the Department of Defense. We thank Brian Persons and Michael Decker for connecting us with Navy and Marines stakeholders, respectively. We thank Laura Werber for valuable input on qualitative analysis methods, and Philip Anton for stepping up to help on short notice on multiple occasions. We appreciate the input we received from several RAND colleagues: Michael Kennedy, Sherrill Lingel, Andrew Lohn, Igor Mikolic-Torreira, George Nacouzi, Caolionn O'Connell, and Steven Popper. We thank our former RAND colleagues, J. Michael Gilmore and Jia Xu, for their helpful perspectives. We thank Susan Catalano and Kayla Howard for their administrative support of the project. We thank our reviewers for their thoughtful feedback: Frank Kendall, our external reviewer, and Philip Anton, Osonde Osoba, and Laura Werber, our internal RAND reviewers. We thank James Powers, NSRD's research quality assurance manager, for his oversight of the review process. Finally, we thank the Acquisition and Technology Policy Center leadership team, Joel Predd and Marjory Blumenthal, for their enthusiasm.

While we acknowledge the contributions of all the above, we remain solely responsible for the quality, integrity, and objectivity of our assessment and recommendations.

Abbreviations

AFC	Army Futures Command
AFMC	Air Force Materiel Command
AFRL	Air Force Research Laboratory
AI	artificial intelligence
ARL	Army Research Laboratory
ARPA	Advanced Research Projects Agency
C3I	command, control, communications, and intelligence
CAPE	Office of Cost Assessment and Program Evaluation
CDO	chief data officer
CIO	chief information officer
CMU	Carnegie Mellon University
CONOPs	concepts of operations
CS	computer science
DARPA	Defense Advanced Research Projects Agency
DIB	Defense Innovation Board

DIU	Defense Innovation Unit
DL	deep learning
DMAG	Deputy's Management Action Group
DoD	U.S. Department of Defense
DoDI	DoD Instruction
DRL	deep reinforcement learning
DSD	Deputy Secretary of Defense
FFRDC	federally funded research and development center
FY	fiscal year
FYDP	Future Years Defense Program
GPS	Global Positioning System
ISR	intelligence, surveillance, and reconnaissance
IT	information technology
JAIC	Joint Artificial Intelligence Center
JCF	Joint Common Foundation
JCIDS	Joint Capabilities Integration and Development System
JROC	Joint Requirements Oversight Council
ML	machine learning
NDAA	National Defense Authorization Act
NDRI	National Defense Research Institute
NDS	National Defense Strategy

NIST	National Institute of Standards and Technologies
NMI	National Mission Initiative
NRL	Naval Research Laboratory
NSF	National Science Foundation
NSIN	National Security Innovation Network
NSTC	National Science and Technology Council
OPM	Office of Personnel Management
OSD	Office of the Secretary of Defense
PB	President's Budget
PCA	principal cyber advisor
PM	predictive maintenance
PPBE	planning, programing, budget and execution system
R&D	research and development
RDT&E	research, development, testing, and evaluation
SAF/AQ	Office of the Assistant Secretary of the Air Force for Acquisition, Technology, and Logistics
SCO	Strategic Capabilities Office
SCP	Strategic Computing Program
SecDevOps	secure development operations
SME	subject-matter expert
SRG	Survey Research Group

SWAP	Software Acquisition and Practices
T&E	testing and evaluation
TTPs	tactics, techniques, and procedures
UAS	unmanned aircraft systems
USD(A&S)	Under Secretary of Defense for Acquisition and Sustainment
USD(I)	Under Secretary of Defense for Intelligence
USD(R&E)	Under Secretary of Defense for Research and Engineering
V&V	verification and validation
VVT&E	verification, validation, testing, and evaluation

CHAPTER ONE

Introduction

This report describes a study, which commenced in December 2018, conducted at a time of heightened national and worldwide interest in artificial intelligence (AI) as a potentially disruptive technology and against the backdrop of the 2018 National Defense Strategy (NDS), which identified long-term strategic competitions with China and Russia as the principal priorities for the U.S. Department of Defense (DoD).[1] We describe the context for this heightened interest in AI by surveying a selection of recent relevant activities within the federal government, including the mandate for this report. This RAND Corporation National Defense Research Institute (NDRI) study was conducted with the awareness of, but largely independent from, these activities. Although our work was informed by existing plans and studies, our analysis and recommendations are not constrained by them.

Study Context

In October 2016, the National Science and Technology Council (NSTC)[2] within the executive branch released two reports on AI that

---

[1] U.S. Department of Defense, *Summary of the 2018 National Defense Strategy of the United States of America: Sharpening the American Military's Competitive Edge*, Washington, D.C., 2018d, p. 3.

[2] The NSTC is a Cabinet-level council within the executive branch, established on November 23, 1993, that sets national goals for federal science and technology investments and coordinates science and technology policy across the federal research and development enterprise.

were developed by the NSTC's Subcommittee on Machine Learning and Artificial Intelligence. The first report surveyed the state of AI and its existing and potential applications and provided 23 recommendations, which covered the federal government and the public sector and addressed AI regulation, research, workforce, governance, and security.[3] The second report laid down a national AI research and development (R&D) strategic plan.[4] In May 2018, the NSTC announced—at the White House Summit on Artificial Intelligence for American Industry—the establishment of the Select Committee on Artificial Intelligence, whose purpose is to advise and assist the NSTC in improving the effectiveness and productivity of federal AI R&D efforts, with a charter ending on December 31, 2020.[5] The National AI R&D Strategic Plan was subsequently updated in June 2019.[6]

Meanwhile, in DoD, then–Deputy Secretary of Defense (DSD) Patrick Shanahan announced in a memorandum the establishment of the Joint Artificial Intelligence Center (JAIC).[7] In July 2018, DoD asked the Defense Innovation Board (DIB)[8] to undertake an effort to spur dialogue and establish a set of principles for the ethical use of AI. The DIB Science and Technology Subcommittee subsequently held a series of three roundtable discussions and public listening sessions in

---

[3]   National Science and Technology Council and Office of Science and Technology Policy, *Preparing for the Future of Artificial Intelligence*, Washington, D.C.: Executive Office of the President, October 2016b.

[4]   National Science and Technology Council and Office of Science and Technology Policy, *The National Artificial Intelligence Research and Development Strategic Plan*, Washington, D.C.: Executive Office of the President, October 2016a.

[5]   Executive Office of the President, *Charter of the National Science and Technology Council Select Committee on Artificial Intelligence*, Washington, D.C., 2018.

[6]   Select Committee on Artificial Intelligence of the National Science and Technology Council, *The National Artificial Intelligence Research and Development Strategic Plan: 2019 Update*, Washington, D.C.: Executive Office of the President, June 2019.

[7]   Deputy Secretary of Defense, "Establishment of the Joint Artificial Intelligence Center," memorandum to military staff, Washington, D.C.: U.S. Department of Defense, June 27, 2018.

[8]   The DIB is a federal advisory committee, set up in 2016, whose mission is to provide the Secretary of Defense, the DSD, and other DoD senior leaders with independent advice and recommendations on innovative means to address future challenges focusing on people and culture, technology and capabilities, and practices and operations.

January, March, and April of 2019. The DIB introduced proposed AI principles and voted to approve them in its October 31, 2019, quarterly public meeting.[9]

The 2019 National Defense Authorization Act (NDAA) was signed into law on August 13, 2018.[10] It contained two pieces of legislation on AI: Section 238, to which this study report pertains, and Section 1051, which legislates the establishment of the National Security Commission on Artificial Intelligence. We shall return to both shortly in our narrative.

The Intelligence Community released the Augmenting Intelligence using Machines (AIM) initiative strategy in January 2019.[11] The AIM initiative outlines four primary investment objectives—one each for the immediate, short, medium, and long terms—to enable the Intelligence Community to fundamentally change the way it produces intelligence.

The presidential executive order on Maintaining American Leadership in AI was signed on February 11, 2019.[12] The executive order emphasizes the paramount importance of continued American leadership in AI for U.S. economic and national security and for shaping the global evolution of AI in a manner consistent with U.S. values, principles, and priorities. In concert with the signing of the executive order, DoD released an unclassified summary of its AI strategy; the strategy outlines a five-pronged strategic approach for delivering AI-enabled capabilities, scaling AI's impact across DoD, cultivating an AI workforce, engaging with allies and partners, and leading in military

---

[9] Defense Innovation Board, *AI Principles: Recommendations on the Ethical Use of Artificial Intelligence by the Department of Defense*, undated a.

[10] Public Law 115–232, John S. McCain National Defense Authorization Act for Fiscal Year 2019, August 13, 2018.

[11] Office of the Director of National Intelligence, *The AIM Initiative: A Strategy for Augmenting Intelligence Using Machines*, Washington, D.C., January 16, 2019.

[12] Donald J. Trump, *Executive Order on Maintaining American Leadership in Artificial Intelligence*, Washington, D.C.: The White House, February 11, 2019.

ethics and AI safety.[13] The strategy also designated the JAIC as the "focal point of the DoD AI Strategy" to "accelerate the delivery of AI-enabled capabilities, scale DoD-wide impact of AI, and synchronize DoD AI activities to expand Joint Force advantage."[14]

More recently, the National Security Commission (NSC)[15] on AI held its first plenary session in March 2019 and released its preliminary report to Congress in July 2019. The NSC has since released its interim report on AI on November 4, 2019.[16]

The DIB released its Software Acquisition and Practices (SWAP) study on May 3, 2019.[17] The military services developed their AI strategy annexes to supplement DoD's AI strategy. DoD released its Digital Modernization Strategy on July 12, 2019; its objective is to support the implementation of the National Defense Strategy via priority initiatives in the cloud; AI; command, control, and communications; and cybersecurity.[18]

The National Institute of Standards and Technology (NIST) released its own AI plan on August 9, 2019, in response to the presiden-

---

[13] U.S. Department of Defense, *Summary of the 2018 Department of Defense Artificial Intelligence Strategy: Harnessing AI to Advance Our Security and Prosperity*, Washington, D.C., 2018c, p. 9.

[14] U.S. Department of Defense, 2018c, p. 9.

[15] The NSC on AI was legislated in Section 1051 of the fiscal year (FY) 2019 NDAA. The NSC is bipartisan, with 15 commissioners appointed by members of Congress and by the Secretaries of Defense and Commerce. It is organized into four working groups focused on: "maintaining U.S. global leadership in AI research," "maintaining global leadership in national security AI application," "preparing our citizens for an AI future," and "ensuring international competitiveness and cooperation in AI" (Public Law 115–232).

[16] National Security Commission on Artificial Intelligence, *Initial Report*, Washington, D.C., July 31, 2019a; National Security Commission on Artificial Intelligence, *Interim Report*, Washington, D.C., November 2019b.

[17] Defense Innovation Board, *Software Is Never Done: Refactoring the Acquisition Code for Competitive Advantage*, 2019a.

[18] U.S. Department of Defense, Office of Publication and Security Review, *DoD Digital Modernization Strategy: DOD Information Resource Management Strategic Plan FY19–23*, Washington, D.C., July 12, 2019.

tial executive order on AI.[19] And the Department of Energy announced the establishment of a departmental Artificial Intelligence and Technology Office on September 6, 2019.[20]

The flurry of activities of the past three years follows extensive interest in autonomy—a capability enabled by advances in AI—within DoD over the past decade. That interest is shown in the numerous studies carried out by the Defense Science Board (DSB)'s[21] Task Force on Countering Autonomy;[22] the now-defunct Naval Research Advisory Committee (NRAC);[23] and the Army Science Board (ASB),[24] which is currently conducting a study on battlefield uses of AI. AI also permeates several of the Air Force Science Advisory Board (SAB)'s recent studies.[25]

---

[19] National Institute of Standards and Technology, *U.S. Leadership in AI: A Plan for Federal Engagement in Developing Technical Standards and Related Tools*, U.S. Department of Commerce, August 9, 2019.

[20] U.S. Department of Energy, "Secretary Perry Stands Up Office for Artificial Intelligence and Technology," September 6, 2019.

[21] The DSB is a federal advisory committee established to provide independent advice to the Secretary of Defense. The DSB maintains a Task Force on Counter Autonomy that issued two reports in 2012 and 2016 and is due to issue a third in late 2019.

[22] U.S. Department of Defense and the Defense Science Board, *Task Force Report: The Role of Autonomy in DoD Systems*, Washington, D.C., July 2012.

[23] The NRAC was an independent civilian scientific advisory group dedicated to providing objective analyses in science, research, and development. It was established in 1946 and disestablished in 2019 and, while it existed, was the senior scientific advisory group to the Secretary of the Navy, the Chief of Naval Operations, the commandant of the Marine Corps, and the Chief of Naval Research. See U.S. Naval Research Advisory Committee, *Autonomous and Unmanned Systems in the Department of the Navy*, September 2017; and U.S. Naval Research Advisory Committee, *Naval Research Advisory Committee Report: How Autonomy Can Transform Naval Operations*, Washington, D.C.; Office of the Secretary of the Navy, October 2012.

[24] The ASB is a federal advisory committee that provides the Army with independent advice and recommendations on matters relating to the Army's scientific, technical, manufacturing, logistics, and business management functions, and other matters deemed pressing or complex by the Secretary of the Army (Army Science Board, *Robotic and Autonomous Systems of Systems Architecture*, Department of the Army, January 15, 2017).

[25] The SAB is a federal advisory committee that reports directly to the Secretary of the Air Force and the Chief of Staff of the Air Force and provides independent advice on science

Of course, DoD's history with AI did not begin in the past year or decade. Its research engagement might be best recognized by the work of the Defense Advanced Research Projects Agency (DARPA),[26] which has been supporting research in AI for more than five decades,[27] and other such DoD components as the Office of Naval Research, the Air Force Office of Scientific Research, and the Army Research Laboratory (ARL), which also have long histories supporting AI research. In September 2018, DARPA announced a $2 billion, multiyear investment in new and existing programs under the banner of the "AI Next" campaign, focusing on advancing new capabilities, robust AI, adversarial AI, high-performance AI, and next-generation AI. In conjunction with the AI Next campaign, DARPA hosted an AI Colloquium in March 2019.

With this context in mind, we now turn our attention to the genesis and objectives of this report.

Study Background and Objectives

Section 238 of the FY 2019 NDAA required the Secretary of Defense to establish a set of activities within DoD to coordinate the department's efforts to develop, mature, and transition AI technologies into operational use, and to designate a senior DoD official as principally responsible for this coordination. It set forth the duties of this designated senior official to include the development of a strategic plan, and

---

and technology relating to the Air Force mission (U.S. Air Force Scientific Advisory Board, *Maintaining Technology Superiority for the United States Air Force (MTS)*, Washington, D.C.: Department of the Air Force, 2018; U.S. Air Force Scientific Advisory Board, *Enhanced Utility of Unmanned Aerial Vehicles in Contested and Denied Environments*, Washington, D.C.: Department of the Air Force, 2015).

[26] DARPA is a DoD agency, created in 1958, that directly reports to the Under Secretary of Defense for Research and Engineering (USD[R&E]) and whose mission is making pivotal investments in breakthrough technologies for national security.

[27] Defense Advanced Research Projects Agency, *DARPA: Defense Advanced Research Projects Agency 1958-2018*, Tampa, Fla.: Faircount Media Group, 2018.

Box 1.1. Text of FY 2019 NDAA Section 238(e)—Study on Artificial Intelligence Topics

(1) IN GENERAL.—Not later than one year after the date of the enactment of this Act, the official designated under subsection (b) shall—

(A) complete a study on past and current advances in artificial intelligence and the future of the discipline, including the methods and means necessary to advance the development of the discipline, to comprehensively address the national security needs and requirements of the Department; and

(B) submit to the congressional defense committees a report on the findings of the designated official with respect to the study completed under subparagraph (A).

(2) CONSULTATION WITH EXPERTS.—In conducting the study required by paragraph (1)(A), the designated official shall consult with experts within the Department, other Federal agencies, academia, any advisory committee established by the Secretary that the Secretary determines appropriate based on the duties of the advisory committee and the expertise of its members, and the commercial sector, as the Secretary considers appropriate.

(3) ELEMENTS.—The study required by paragraph (1)(A) shall include the following:

(A) A comprehensive and national-level review of—

(i) advances in artificial intelligence, machine learning, and associated technologies relevant to the needs of the Department and the Armed Forces; and

(ii) the competitiveness of the Department in artificial intelligence, machine learning, and such technologies.

(B) Near-term actionable recommendations to the Secretary for the Department to secure and maintain technical advantage in artificial intelligence, including ways—

(i) to more effectively organize the Department for artificial intelligence;

(ii) to educate, recruit, and retain leading talent; and

(iii) to most effectively leverage investments in basic and advanced research and commercial progress in these technologies.

Box 1.1—Continued

(C) Recommendations on the establishment of Departmentwide data standards and the provision of incentives for the sharing of open training data, including those relevant for research into systems that integrate artificial intelligence and machine learning with human teams.

(D) Recommendations for engagement by the Department with relevant agencies that will be involved with artificial intelligence in the future.

(E) Recommendations for legislative action relating to artificial intelligence, machine learning, and associated technologies, including recommendations to more effectively fund and organize the Department.

SOURCE: Pub. L. 115–232, 2018.

mandated in Section 238(e) that this official carry out a study on AI topics. The language of Section 238(e) is reproduced in Box 1.1.

In December 2018, Lieutenant General Jack Shanahan, director of the JAIC, asked RAND NDRI to conduct a study to independently assess DoD's posture in AI in the spirit of Section 238(e). Shanahan has since (as of October 2019) been designated as the senior DoD official with principal responsibility for DoD-wide AI coordination.

On January 11, 2019, the principal investigator of this study and other RAND personnel met with the congressional staffers responsible for the drafting of the NDAA. The objective of the meeting was to understand the genesis and objectives of Section 238(e). We were explicitly advised that the review of the "competitiveness of [DoD] in artificial intelligence, machine learning, and such technologies"[28] (see Box 1.1) should be an *introspective* independent review, seeking to assess whether DoD is correctly postured to be a builder and buyer of these technologies, rather than a review relative to near-peer com-

---

[28] Pub. L. 115–232, 2018.

petitors as the language seems to suggest.[29] We were further advised that we should design and conduct this posture assessment in a way that will enable our approach and structure to be applicable to future posture assessments of other technologies. Moreover, we were advised that the desired review of "advances in artificial intelligence, machine learning, and associated technologies relevant to the needs of [DoD] and the Armed Forces"[30] (see Box 1.1) should remain at the "above program level" and should not lead to yet another report on current AI technologies or potential uses of AI technologies in DoD, about which they had plenty of reports, though perhaps more "myth busting" would be in order, according to staffers. Finally, the staffers emphasized that we should be conducting an *independent* assessment.

Accordingly, in line with this guidance, we distilled the congressional language to formulate the following three objectives for our study:

1. Assess the state of AI relevant to DoD and address misconceptions.
2. Carry out an independent introspective assessment of DoD's posture for AI.[31]
3. Develop a set of recommendations for internal DoD actions, external engagements, and potential legislative or regulatory actions to enhance DoD's posture in AI.

This report is aimed at a broad congressional, DoD, and interested public audience with varied technical knowledge. As a result, we strive to describe our findings and recommendations as clearly as

---

[29] Likewise, the guidance we received from our sponsor emphasized that the assessment should be an introspective look at DoD, rather than a look at competitive posture relative to near peers.

[30] Pub. L. 115–232, 2018.

[31] As we shall see in Chapter Two, and in line with the guidance received from the congressional staffers, our assessment of DoD's posture is wide-ranging, going beyond technology or strategy to incorporate *almost all* elements necessary for DoD's scaling of AI. The only notable exception is ethical principles and guidelines, which were explicitly excluded from the scope of our study per sponsor guidance in view of the DIB's mandate to address them.

possible and to provide sufficient context to reach the widest possible audience while remaining true to important technological or organizational details.

Organization of This Report

This report is organized as follows. In Chapter Two, we summarize the analytical approach and methodology employed in this study. To avoid interrupting the flow of the report, we have opted to relegate the details of the methodology to Appendix A. In Chapter Three, we discuss our findings regarding the state of AI, particularly those that are most relevant to DoD. We present in Chapter Four our assessment of DoD's current posture in AI, and we highlight, in particular, the obstacles and friction points we have observed. In Chapter Five, we conclude with a set of recommendations to enhance DoD's posture, and we connect those recommendations to the appropriate elements of the 2019 NDAA. We supplement our report with a summary of relevant insights gleaned from our extensive interviews with government officials, in Appendix B; insights from academia and industry, in Appendix C; and insights from our selection of historical case studies, in Appendix D. In Appendix E, we collect a selection of publicly available definitions of AI, and we revisit our interviewees' conceptualization of AI and the desirability of a DoD-wide definition of AI. An associated annex, which is not available to the public, outlines the analytic approach, findings, and recommendations of our independent review of DoD's portfolio of AI investments.

CHAPTER TWO

Analytical Framework and Methodology

Six Dimensions for Posture Assessment

The starting point of our study was the underlying premise, implicit in the language of Section 238(e) of the 2019 NDAA, that DoD needs to posture for "artificial intelligence," notwithstanding uncertainty about the intended definition of that term. Indeed, although Section 238(g) of the NDAA proposed a definition of the term for the purpose of the legislation (Appendix E), it simultaneously required (in Section 238[f]) the Secretary of Defense to define the term for use within DoD. We shall return to the question of defining AI in Chapter Three.

Motivated, in part, by the desire to remain agnostic to the precise definition of AI, we cast a wide net at the outset of the study and asked the question: If we want to assess DoD's ability to build or acquire, test, transition, and sustain, at scale,[1] a set of far-reaching technologies falling under the broad AI umbrella, what dimensions of posture should we be investigating and assessing? Based on guidance from congressional staffers and the sponsor, and careful consideration and deliberation within the research team, we distilled the information needed to answer this question into six dimensions that formed the analytical framework for our posture assessment. For simplicity, we denote each of these six dimensions by a single word title, though each dimen-

---

[1]   The term *at scale* refers to moving beyond technology demonstrations, prototypes, pilots, and isolated uses to deployment of AI to its full potential across DoD. We will return to a discussion of the implications and challenges of scaling AI in Chapter Three.

sion, in reality, encompasses a variety of related considerations. The six dimensions are defined as follows:

Organization: The executive-level strategic view of DoD's posture, composed of the vision, strategy, and resource commitments; the organizational structures to support this vision; and the stakeholders and their mandates, authorities, and roles.

Advancement: Research, development, and prototyping to advance the state of the technology, and frameworks, approaches, and tools to verify, validate, test, and evaluate the technologies as they develop and mature.

Adoption: All aspects of the procurement, fielding, sustainment, and life-cycle management of mature technologies, and the redesign of doctrine; concepts of operations (CONOPs); tactics, techniques, and procedures (TTPs); and business or other processes for best use of these technologies.

Innovation: Both the internal culture for innovation and the various avenues and mechanisms for bringing external innovations or innovators into DoD.

Data: A broad AI-specific dimension that encompasses data as a resource; the governance rules and policies that surround its collection and use; and the storage, computational, communication, and other technical infrastructure needed to leverage the data at scale.

Talent: The talent needed to develop, acquire, sustain, and operate these technologies; and the mechanisms for recruiting, retaining, cultivating, and growing such talent at various stages of their careers.

With the exception of the data dimension, which speaks to the specifics of recent advances in AI techniques, every other dimension we propose for our posture assessment could be used to assess DoD's posture for any other technology, digital or otherwise. Therefore, our analytical framework follows the guidance given by congressional staffers (see Chapter One).

For ease of reference, we summarize these six dimensions in Table 2.1 and organize them according to theme: the *executive view*; the *execution* of the goal of building or acquiring, testing, transitioning, and sustaining the technologies at scale; and the *enablers* necessary to succeed in this goal.

Table 2.1
Analytical Framework for Our DoD Posture Assessment

Theme	Dimension	Components
Executive view	Organization	• Vision, strategy, and resource commitments • Organizational structures • Stakeholders and their mandates, authorities, and roles
Execution	Advancement	• R&D portfolio and activities • Prototyping • Verification, validation, testing, and evaluation (VVT&E)
	Adoption	• Procurement • Fielding, sustainment, and life-cycle management • Development of doctrine, CONOPs, TTPs, and processes
Enablers	Innovation	• Internal culture of innovation • Mechanisms for leveraging external innovations • Mechanisms for engaging external innovators
	Data	• Data as a resource • Governance of data collection and use • Storage, computing, and other infrastructure
	Talent	• Talent needed to develop, acquire, sustain, and operate • Recruitment, retention, cultivation, and growth • Career management

In describing the analytical framework for our posture assessment, we would be remiss if we omitted that DoD carried out two recent posture assessments, specifically the 2018 Nuclear Posture Review and the 2018 DoD Cyber Strategy and Cyber Posture Review,[2] which informed DoD's updated 2018 Cyber Strategy. The summary of this strategy is publicly available.[3] Both of these posture reviews included a major

---

[2] U.S. Department of Defense, "Fact Sheet: 2018 DoD Cyber Strategy and Cyber Posture Review," Washington, D.C., 2018a; U.S. Department of Defense, *Nuclear Posture Review*, Washington, D.C., February 2018b.

[3] U.S. Department of Defense, *Summary: Department of Defense Cyber Strategy*, Washington, D.C., 2018e.

focus on threat assessment and assessments relative to near-peer competitors, and therefore diverged significantly from our mandate of an introspective assessment and our corresponding analytical framework.

Another recent introspective DoD review was the Cybersecurity Readiness Review that the Department of the Navy undertook following the loss of significant amounts of data.[4] In view of its narrower focus on cybersecurity governance following a specific set of incidents, the study focus and approach were more narrowly scoped than those of our report, even while we note elements of overlap in the analytical framework (e.g., consideration of organizational structure and talent) and analytic methodology (e.g., the use of interviews within and outside DoD as a data collection method, as we describe in the following section).

Overview of the Analytic Methodology

In view of the breadth and dimensions of the assessment, the desire for extensive and varied input per the congressional language, and the bounded period of the study,[5] we assembled a multidisciplinary team of researchers, analysts, and staff,[6] and we initiated four data collection and analysis efforts that proceeded roughly in parallel. The first three efforts were exploratory, aiming for a qualitative view of the landscape from multiple perspectives. These efforts were followed by an integrative analysis to distill emerging themes across multiple data sources.

---

[4] Secretary of the Navy, *Cybersecurity Readiness Review*, Washington, D.C.: Department of the Navy, March 4, 2019.

[5] The original deadline for submission of this report to Congress was August 13, 2019. This deadline was extended, after a request from DoD, to November 26, 2019, thereby allowing an effective study period of nine months. The work of the RAND NDRI study team commenced on December 21, 2018.

[6] A noteworthy aspect is the breadth of expertise in the RAND NDRI study team. Indeed, the relevant collective technical expertise of the team spanned control theory, machine learning (ML), optimization, game theory, software engineering, and quantum physics. The collective nontechnical expertise of the team spanned acquisition, organizational change management, and talent management. The collective professional experience of the team spanned government (including DoD), academia, and industry.

The fourth effort was a quantitative assessment of DoD's current AI investment portfolio. These four lines of effort can be summarized as follows:

- *Government interviews:* We conducted 68 semistructured interviews and discussions with stakeholders and subject-matter experts (SMEs) from DoD and other federal agencies and advisory bodies (Table 2.2). The primary goals of this exploratory effort were to understand current DoD activities in AI, and, in particular, to understand the obstacles faced and the points of friction encountered and the AI activities within other relevant federal agencies and organizations. A secondary goal was to understand lessons learned from the federal experience with AI outside DoD.
- *Academic and industry interviews:* We conducted 34 semistructured interviews and discussions with leaders and SMEs in top-ranked academic institutions and in industry, both in the technology industry and beyond (Table 2.3). The primary goals of this exploratory effort were to understand the DoD-relevant state of AI, its limitations, and its projected path (to the extent possible), and the lessons learned and best practices from the people advancing, adopting, and scaling AI outside the government. A secondary goal was to explore existing and potential partnerships between DoD and these organizations and entities in academia and industry.
- *Historical case studies:* We selected and carried out six historical case studies covering DoD's prior experience with AI and DoD's experience adopting and scaling other technologies, both digital and otherwise. The primary goal of this exploratory effort was to understand the lessons learned—positive and negative—from DoD's own history with technology at scale, to complement the insights gleaned from consultation with experts, as was mandated by the congressional language and carried out through the interviews described in the first two lines of effort.
- *Portfolio review:* We carried out a review of DoD's investment portfolio in AI, using raw data we received from the President's Budget (PB) 2019 and PB 2020 data calls from the Office of Cost

Table 2.2
Organizational Affiliations of Federal Interviewees

	Organizations
Department of Defense	
Office of the Secretary of Defense (OSD)	• DARPA • Defense Innovation Unit (DIU) • JAIC • National Security Innovation Network (NSIN) • Office of Cost Assessment and Program Evaluation • Office of the Chief Data Officer (CDO) • Office of the Chief Information Officer (CIO) • Office of the Under Secretary of Defense for Acquisition and Sustainment (USD [A&S]) • Office of the Under Secretary of Defense for Intelligence (USD[I]) • Office of the Under Secretary of Defense for Personnel and Readiness • Office of the USD(R&E) • Strategic Capabilities Office (SCO)
Combatant commands	• Transportation Command
Air Force	• Air Force Materiel Command (AFMC) • Air Force Research Laboratory (AFRL) • Office of the CDO • Office of the CIO • Office of Deputy Chief of Staff/Manpower & Personnel (A1) • Office of Deputy Chief of Staff/Intelligence, Surveillance, and Reconnaissance (A2) • Office of Deputy Chief of Staff/Operations, Plans, and Requirements (A3) • Office of Studies & Analyses, Assessments, and Lessons Learned (A9) • Office of Assistant Secretary of the Air Force/Acquisition (SAF/AQ) • Office of the Secretary of the Air Force/ Chief of Staff of the Air Force (SECAF/CSAF)
Army	• Army Futures Command (AFC) • ARL • Office of the Assistant Secretary of the Army for Acquisition, Logistics, and Technology • Office of the CIO • Office of the Deputy Chief of Staff for Personnel (G-1) • Office of the Deputy Chief of Staff for Programs (G-8)

Table 2.2—Continued

	Organizations
Marines	• Office of the Deputy Commandant Capabilities Development and Integration • Office of the Deputy Commandant Manpower and Reserve Affairs • Office of the Deputy Commandant Information
Navy	• Office of the Director for Innovation, Technology Requirements and Test & Evaluation (OPNAV N94) • Office of Naval Research • Naval Research Laboratory (NRL) • Office of the Deputy Assistant Secretary of the Navy for C4I/Information Operations/Space • Office of the CIO • Office of the Chief Management Officer • Office of the Deputy Chief of Naval Operations for Manpower, Personnel, Training, and Education (OPNAV N1) • Office of the Deputy Chief of Naval Operations for Information Dominance (OPNAV N2/N6)
Non–DoD	
Federal advisory boards	• National Security Commission on AI
Federal government and federal agencies	• Intelligence Advanced Research Projects Activity • National Science Foundation (NSF) • NIST • Office of Management and Budget • Office of Science and Technology Policy

Assessment and Program Evaluation. The objective of our review was to assess the overall resources committed, their horizon, and the general characteristics of the portfolio. The availability of program-level raw data helped in undertaking a quantitative analysis, allowing us to assess DoD's current posture as exemplified by the investments it is currently making in AI. The details of the portfolio review—including methodology, findings, and recommendations—are in a separate annex to this report that is not available to the general public.

Each of the first three lines of effort aimed to cover all six dimensions of the posture assessment, thereby providing insights and inputs

Table 2.3
Organizational Affiliations of Academic and Industry Interviewees

Interview Group	Organizational Affiliations
Academic institutions	• California Institute of Technology • Carnegie Mellon University • Cornell Tech • Georgia Institute of Technology • Massachusetts Institute of Technology • Stanford University • University of California, Berkeley
Industry: technology firms	• Amazon • IBM • Microsoft • NVIDIA • Palantir Technologies
Industry: defense industrial base	• The Boeing Company • General Dynamics Corporation • Lockheed Martin Corporation • United Technologies Corporation
Industry: strategy consulting firms	• Boston Consulting Group • McKinsey & Company
Industry: hospitals	• Cleveland Clinic • Beth Israel Deaconess Medical Center
Industry: investment banks	• Goldman Sachs • J.P. Morgan • Morgan Stanley

into each dimension from three separate types of sources. Moreover, we used two additional sources to complement these lines of effort: First, and particularly where the state of AI assessment was concerned, we drew on the technical expertise in the team. Second, we drew on the published literature opportunistically as the study progressed, to provide additional input on all six dimensions of the posture assessment.

We then merged the three exploratory lines of effort (supplemented by consultation of the relevant literature and the expertise of the study team) to parse, organize, and evaluate the inputs collected along each of the six dimensions of our analytical framework. Therefore, we were able to synthesize an emerging picture of the state of the technology and its DoD implications, DoD's current activities and an assessment of its posture along the six dimensions, the lessons learned from experiences with AI outside DoD, and past DoD experience with AI and other technologies. From this integrated picture across the varied data sources, we distilled a set of recommendations that we believe will be both actionable and impactful in enhancing DoD's posture.

In contrast, the fourth line of effort was, for the most part, a stand-alone effort primarily addressing the organization (particularly the resource commitments), advancement, and adoption dimensions of the posture assessment (particularly the scope and balance of DoD AI technology investments, a question of particular interest for our sponsor). The details of this analytic effort, including selection of the interviewees and case studies, the topics our engagements sought to explore, and the approaches used to organize and analyze the qualitative data we collected are described in Appendix A.

Assumptions and Limitations

A discussion of the analytical framework and methodology would be incomplete without clarifying the assumptions and limitations of our study.

As we noted at the beginning of this chapter, we emphasize that the starting points of our study were the assumptions that DoD needs to posture for AI as a transformational technology, and that therefore DoD should be looking for ways to scale AI, as opposed to adopting a few discrete capabilities that are AI-enabled. The bases for these assumptions were the underlying premise, implicit in the language of Section 238 of the 2019 NDAA, that DoD needs to competitively posture for AI,[7] and DIB's Technology and Capabilities Recommendation 5, which characterized AI and ML as presenting transformational capabilities to DoD.[8]

The findings and analysis we report had several limitations. First, the breadth of the study had natural implications for depth. Indeed,

---

[7]   Pub. L. 115–232, 2018.

[8]   Defense Innovation Board, "Our Work: Recommendations," webpage, undated b.

although each of the dimensions of our posture assessment could have been the subject of an in-depth study of its own, these in-depth studies were not pursued because the main objective was to carry out a broad assessment at the strategic level. Additionally, because of the breadth of the topic and constraints on time and resources, we had to carefully choose a subset of organizations and SMEs to interview at the federal level. We prioritized interviewees who would enable us to understand the AI activities and landscape within OSD and the services across our six dimensions of posture assessment. Therefore, we did not interview some other federal entities, notably national labs and the Intelligence Community. We also did not interview federally funded research and development centers (FFRDCs) and university-affiliated research centers, both of which might have had something to contribute. Moreover, although the selection and outreach to interviewees were done systemically in accordance with the stated objectives of the study, there is the potential for sample bias, particularly as completed interviews were partially influenced by access and availability. This was particularly the case for industry, including the defense industrial base, where we would have liked to cast a wider net but were limited by our ability to secure interviews.

The government interviews were conducted between April 3, 2019, and August 29, 2019. We have no reason to believe that the emergent themes, findings, and recommendations regarding DoD's posture for AI are affected by DoD activity in the intervening period. However, since interviews were conducted, the status of certain DoD initiatives might have evolved in ways that are not reflected in this report.

CHAPTER THREE

The DoD-Relevant State of Artificial Intelligence

In this chapter, we present our assessment of the state of AI as it pertains to DoD. In doing so, we address some common misconceptions in line with staffer guidance (see Chapter One), and set realistic expectations. Because considerable confusion can arise from differing views of what constitutes AI, we begin by considering the question of what AI is, and whether DoD would benefit from a unified, DoD-wide definition of AI. We then propose a conceptual framework that lays out the dimensions that should be considered when thinking about AI and its relevance to DoD's unique mission and needs. Finally, we summarize for decisionmakers what we believe they need to know about the state of AI within this conceptual framework, while keeping the discussion at a high level ("above program level") in line with staffer guidance (see Chapter One).

Defining Artificial Intelligence—or Not?

It is outside the scope of our study to define *artificial intelligence*. Nonetheless, we wanted to understand how our interviewees conceptualize the term and whether they believe there is value in establishing a DoD-wide definition of AI. We heard diverse opinions among our federal, industry, and academic interviewees on both questions, with no consensus emerging (see section "Interviewee Input" in Appendix E). This is not surprising: We also collected some of the publicly available (official) definitions of AI (see section "Existing Definitions" in Appendix E) and noted a similar lack of convergence. Indeed, the debate on how to define AI continues unabated decades after the term was first coined.

Overall, devising a good definition of AI is challenging. Defining AI in terms of high-level aspirational goals (e.g., "machines that think" or "computers that perform tasks that normally require human intelligence") is simple, but does not serve any practical purpose, such as helping DoD delineate and evaluate its AI investments, or articulate and assess its AI talent needs. It also has the unfortunate side effect of feeding the hype around AI—noted, for example, by 2018 Turing co-awardee Yoshua Bengio: "I think it would be a good thing if there's a correction in the business world, because that's where the hype is."[1] Defining AI in terms of specific techniques (e.g., "expert systems" or "deep learning [DL]") is elusive, as history has taught us that what constitutes AI changes significantly with time and perspective; this is noted in DARPA's perspective on the three waves of AI (see section "Existing Definitions: DARPA" in Appendix E). Defining AI in terms of specific capabilities (e.g., "object recognition in imagery") is likewise problematic because of the rapid pace of technological change and the inherent difficulties in anticipating both the rates and uses of technological advances, as noted in our case studies (see section "AI History in DoD" in Appendix D and section "The Offset Strategy" in Appendix D).

Nonetheless, DoD needs to get a handle on both its AI investments and its AI talent needs and availability. Doing so requires some basic level of agreement on the delineation of AI within DoD for each of these purposes—one that is unlikely to be reached by simply adopting a DoD-wide definition, no matter how carefully crafted.

A Conceptual Framework for DoD AI

We next propose a conceptual framework that remains agnostic to the precise definition of AI while allowing one to think systematically

---

[1] Will Knight, "An AI Pioneer Wants His Algorithms to Understand the 'Why,'" *Wired*, October 8, 2019.

about the intricacies of the *technologies and capabilities space*, the *spectrum of DoD AI applications*, and the *investment space and time horizon* (Figure 3.1). More importantly, this framework allows one to explore the interplay among these three elements, which ultimately affects DoD's success in developing or acquiring AI technologies and scaling their use in support of its mission, and the expected timelines for doing so.

The team developed this conceptual framework by drawing on the technical expertise of its members, but shared broad aspects of it

Figure 3.1
A Conceptual Framework for DoD AI

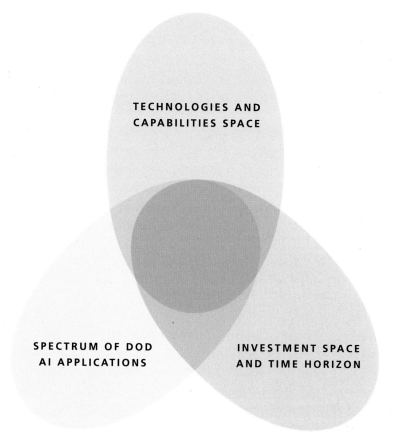

TECHNOLOGIES AND
CAPABILITIES SPACE

SPECTRUM OF DOD
AI APPLICATIONS

INVESTMENT SPACE
AND TIME HORIZON

both with the sponsor during interim progress reviews and with interviewees, thereby providing opportunities for feedback and refinement.

Technologies and Capabilities Space

The first element in our conceptual framework, the *technologies and capabilities space*, covers the theoretical results and methodological approaches—including models, algorithms, and heuristics—that underpin the currently available AI solutions. The technologies and capabilities space also covers the potential capabilities that these AI solutions enable. We will review the prominent recent developments in this space in the following section.

Spectrum of DoD AI Applications

The second element in our conceptual framework covers the *spectrum of applications of AI in support of DoD's mission*, which are notable in scope and breadth. The applications of AI within DoD fall along a spectrum characterized by four independent factors:

- the degree of control one has over the environment in which the AI solution is developed and deployed
- the extent to which relevant resources, including data sets, computational power, and communication bandwidth are expected to be available
- the tempo at which the AI algorithms are expected to process information and provide an output, from slow (order of hours or days) to real time
- the implications of failure of the AI solution, and the potential to recover from such failures when they occur.

This characterization of the spectrum of DoD AI applications is relevant for technologists considering development of AI solutions and the mapping of methodological approaches (i.e., the technologies and capabilities space) to potential applications or use cases (i.e., the spectrum of DoD AI applications). Indeed, it is important to appreciate that these factors will have implications for the feasibility of AI solutions and their expected development timeline. For example, correctly recognizing objects in images in different operating environments and under different resource constraints likely requires different technical approaches: Recognizing cats in pictures downloaded from the web using an algorithm trained on an available labeled data set, such as ImageNet,[2] while sitting in the Pentagon, might require a different approach from recognizing missile launchers in real time on a battlefield from satellite imagery. The former is feasible now, while the latter might not be. Although these two applications might seem very similar to the user, they are not necessarily similar to the technologist or operator.

Importantly, our characterization of the spectrum of DoD AI applications along these four factors can be mapped reasonably well to three broad categories of AI applications, specifically enterprise AI, mission-support AI, and operational AI, as we describe in the following paragraphs.[3] Doing so renders our characterization, and its implications for policymaking, decisionmaking, and realistic expectation-setting intuitively accessible to decisionmakers (Figure 3.2).

Enterprise AI refers to AI applications, typically within the United States, where the environment in which the system is developed and operated is well-controlled and relatively benign; where resources such as data and infrastructure (storage, computation, communication bandwidth) should be available or, in principle, could be made available in ample supply; where the tempo for information-processing and decisionmaking is relatively relaxed; and where, should failures occur, recovering from them should be possible with limited lasting damage. Examples of enterprise AI applications include AI-enabled financial or personnel management systems or AI-enabled management of health care records for service members.

On the other end of the spectrum lie applications that we term *operational AI*: those AI solutions employed in an operating environment that is dynamic, uncertain, adversarial, and partially outside our

---

[2] ImageNet, homepage, undated.

[3] Although the four factors are independent, in practice they tend to vary in tandem, rendering the linear layout of enterprise, mission-support, and operational AI a useful, though imperfect, simplified construct.

Figure 3.2
The Spectrum of DoD AI Applications

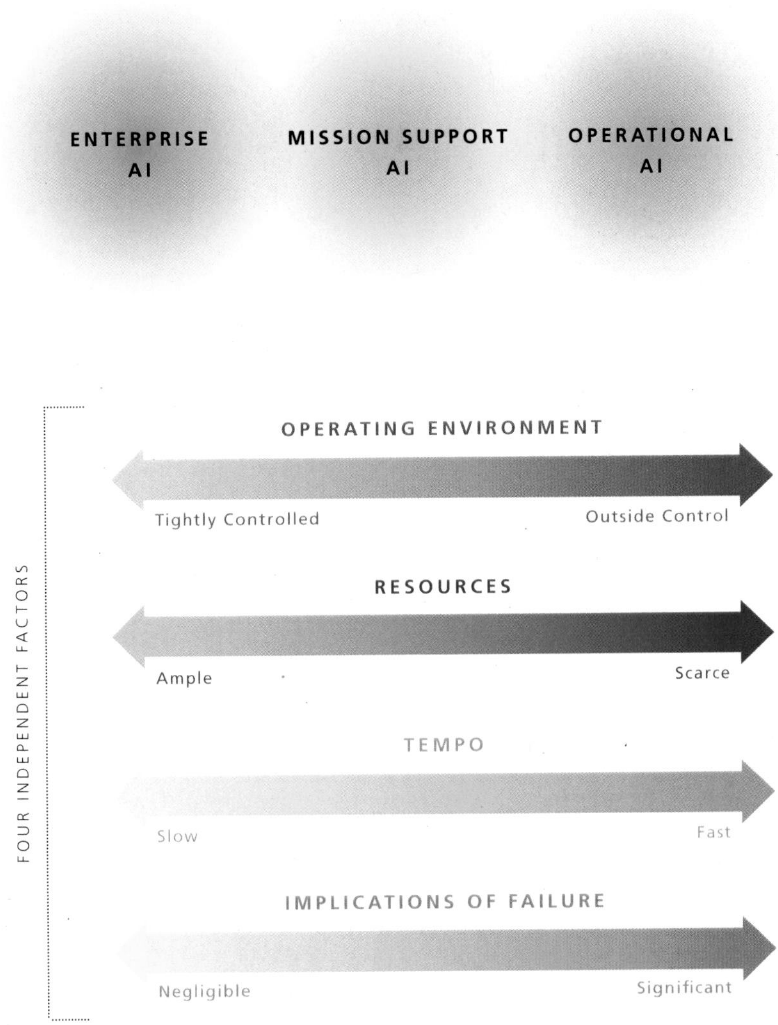

control, where certain resources might be much more limited,[4] where the tempo for information-processing and decisionmaking is expected to be much faster, and where the consequences of failure are expected to be much higher. Examples of operational AI are the Patriot Missile Long-Range Air Defense System, the Aegis Combat System, and the currently pursued Skyborg prototype.[5]

Somewhere in between enterprise AI and operational AI are *mission support AI* applications, such as the Algorithmic Warfare Cross-Functional team (CFT), also known as Project Maven; internet monitoring systems; and AI-enabled logistics planning systems. In particular, Project Maven aims to use ML to assist humans in analyzing large quantities of imagery from full-motion video data collected by drones. Although the data collection occurs in theater, its processing occurs in the United States.[6]

It should be emphasized that these three categories of AI applications lack neatly defined boundaries. Indeed, they are simplified constructs to render consideration of the spectrum of DoD AI applications more intuitive for policymakers and decisionmakers. We have tried to highlight this in Figure 3.2 by representing these three categories as overlapping circles with fuzzy boundaries.

Investment Space and Time Horizon

The final element of our conceptual framework is the investment space and time horizon. Various investments are needed to ensure that DoD appropriately leverages AI. Investments are clearly necessary to develop or acquire the technologies and capabilities that enable AI applications

---

[4]   For example, the availability of high-bandwidth, low-latency communication allowing reach-back to the cloud, or even among devices in the field, might be limited in theater. Likewise, the availability of computation and data storage in theater might be limited. Finally, the availability of relevant data sets to adequately train or retrain AI algorithms might be limited.

[5]   See, for instance, Bryan Ripple, "Skyborg Program Seeks Industry Input for Artificial Intelligence Initiative," U.S. Air Force, webpage, March 27, 2019.

[6]   Zachary Fryer-Biggs, "Inside the Pentagon's Plan to Win Over Silicon Valley's AI Experts," *Wired*, December 21, 2018; Yasmin Tadjdeh, "AI Project to Link Military, Silicon Valley," *National Defense*, February 7, 2019.

across the DoD spectrum of enterprise AI, mission-support AI, and operational AI. Beyond these three obvious buckets of investments, at least three additional types of investments are necessary for advancement and adoption of AI at scale.

The first are investments in a set of technological and other enablers, including infrastructure for storage, computation, and communication; data collection and curation efforts; a secure development operations (SecDevOps) environment integrating development, security, and operations teams;[7] processes for fast, continuous integration; and training for the users and operators.

The second set are investments that underpin and enable technical checks and balances, consisting of verification and validation (V&V) of the AI technology and some form of testing and evaluation (T&E) during the research, development, and deployment phases of the AI solution and throughout its life-cycle.

Additionally, investments in foundational basic research not specifically aligned with a particular product or application (research, development, testing, and evaluation [RDT&E] budget category 6.1, sometimes 6.2) are important to ensure a vigorous pipeline of scientific advances and to maintain technological advantage in the long term. For instance, in a 2015 paper coauthored by the three recipients of the 2018 Association for Computing Machinery Turing Award, the authors state that, "In the late 1990s, neural nets and backpropagation were largely forsaken by the machine-learning community and ignored by the computer-vision and speech-recognition communities."[8] Additionally, "Interest in deep feedforward networks was revived around 2006 . . . by a group of researchers brought together by the Canadian Institute for Advanced Research (CIFAR)."[9] We are now witnessing the outcomes of this revival, with DL credited with major advances in varied fields (described in the following section). Note that such investments in foundational basic research need

---

[7]   Defense Innovation Board, *SWAP Main Report*, Washington, D.C., May 3, 2019b.

[8]   Yann LeCun, Yoshua Bengio, and Geoffrey Hinton, "Deep Learning," *Nature*, Vol. 521, May 28, 2015, p. 438.

[9]   LeCun, Bengio, and Hinton, 2015, p. 439.

not be entirely in DoD accounts but could also draw upon other federal sources, such as the NSF.

The final, critical, consideration we wish to highlight, in conjunction with the investment dimension, is that of time horizons. Time horizons are important for setting ambitious but realistic goals and expectations. For simplicity, and in line with best practices in strategy development gleaned from our industry interviews (see section "Industry: Organization" in Appendix C), we have opted to frame the discussion of time horizons in terms of five-year windows representing the short term (up to five years), middle term (five to ten years), and long term (longer than ten years).

What Decisionmakers Should Know About the DoD-Relevant State of AI

Having laid out our conceptual framework for thinking about DoD AI, we present here our assessment of the current state of AI as it pertains to DoD, focusing, in particular, on answering the following three main questions that we believe are relevant to decisionmakers:

1. What are prominent recent developments in AI?
2. How might these recent AI developments enhance DoD's mission, and what would it take to scale them across DoD applications?
3. What do answers to the first two questions mean for DoD planning?

The answer to the first question effectively summarizes the state of the art pertaining to the technologies and capabilities element in our conceptual framework. The answer to the second question effectively connects the technologies and capabilities space to the spectrum of AI applications at a high level: Per sponsor and congressional staffer guidance (see Chapter One), we did not attempt to delve deeper into potential use cases in this study. Finally, the answer to the third question provides some guidelines to ambitiously but realistically set the goals and expectations regarding DoD AI investments and their expected returns.

Our assessment is based on the synthesis of three sources, specifically the evidence collected in our interviews with technical interviewees in academia, industry, DoD, and other federal government departments and agencies;[10] consultation of the relevant technical literature; and our team's technical expertise.

Prominent Recent Developments in AI Technologies and Capabilities

Many different technical approaches underpin AI, including *ML*, an established field in computer science (CS) consisting of a set of techniques with strong roots in statistics and optimization and that allows one to discover patterns in data.[11] The rate of technological advancement in certain subfields of ML, particularly DL, has been significant over the past decade. DL employs neural-network models with multiple layers to learn representations of complex data.[12] The design and deployment of such algorithms typically consist of a training phase, which involves solving an optimization problem to best fit the model to the training data according to some learning criterion, and an inference phase, in which the trained model is employed to find similar patterns in new data. Because of the complexity of these models, the training phase typically requires large, labeled data sets and extensive computing power, whereas the computing power required in the inference phase is much lower. Typically, this is not a linear one-time process (training, then inference) but a sequence of training and inference phases to enhance or even maintain the algorithm's performance.

---

[10] We include in that group both interviewees in technical roles and interviewees with significant technical backgrounds (science, technology, engineering, and math [STEM] degrees in fields related to AI). Although a majority of our interviewees were in leadership positions, many of them came from technical backgrounds and had strong opinions about the state of technology.

[11] Christopher M. Bishop, *Pattern Recognition and Machine Learning (Information Science and Statistics)*, 2nd ed., New York: Springer, 2011; Trevor Hastie, Robert Tibshirani, and Jerome Friedman, *The Elements of Statistical Learning: Data Mining, Inference, and Prediction*, New York: Springer, 2009, corrected at 12th printing, 2017.

[12] LeCun, Bengio, and Hinton, 2015.

The net result of these advancements is great progress in supervised ML (*supervised* here refers to the use of labeled data sets to train the models), in turn leading to breakthrough progress in tasks involving classification and prediction.[13] Image classification examples are perhaps the most visible to the public, owing to the ImageNet Large Scale Visual Recognition Competition, which is based on the ImageNet data set.[14] Beyond image processing, these advancements have led to similarly significant breakthroughs on some long-standing problems in speech processing and in natural-language processing,[15] with ensuing applications in machine translation and document classification, among others.

Another prominent direction of recent advances is in deep reinforcement learning (DRL). *Reinforcement learning* (RL) is a classical field that,[16] at its core, is about solving sequential decisionmaking problems with deferred rewards in an approximate manner. RL has witnessed a resurgence of interest in the recent past because of the promise of DL techniques to arrive at these approximate solutions.

DRL has led to new breakthroughs in strategy games. For instance, these algorithms have recently beaten world-class champi-

---

[13] Examples of classification tasks include recognizing objects in images, captioning photos, extracting words from speech, and determining the topic of a text.

[14] Olga Russakovsky, Jia Deng, Hao Su, Jonathan Krause, Sanjeev Satheesh, Sean Ma, Zhiheng Huang, Andrej Karpathy, Aditya Khosla, Michael Bernstein, Alexander C. Berg, and Li Fei-Fei, "ImageNet Large Scale Visual Recognition Challenge," *International Journal of Computer Vision*, Vol. 115, No. 3, December 2015; Alex Krizhevsky, Ilya Sutskever, and Geoffrey E. Hinton, "ImageNet Classification with Deep Convolutional Neural Networks," *Communications of the ACM*, Vol. 60, No. 6, June 2017.

[15] Tomas Mikolov, Kai Chen, Greg Corrado, and Jeffrey Dean, "Efficient Estimation of Word Representations in Vector Space," *arXiv:1301.3781*, September 7, 2013.

[16] M. Waltz and K. Fu, "A Heuristic Approach to Reinforcement Learning Control Systems," *IEEE Transactions on Automatic Control*, Vol. 10, No. 4, 1965.

ons at the games of Go,[17] shoji,[18] and Starcraft II, a real-time strategy game.[19] In spite of all the excitement and hype surrounding these developments, it is wise to note the caution expressed by prominent academics in assessing the true significance of these developments. Indeed, training of DRL algorithms appears to be a particularly inefficient process and one with serious reproducibility issues,[20] leading to serious questions about its applicability in real life, beyond simulations and games.[21]

Scaling Recent AI Developments Across DoD Applications

Given the recent technical breakthroughs and advances we described in the previous section, reasonable questions to ask are: How might these new advances enhance DoD's mission, and what would it take to scale them across DoD?[22]

The answer to these questions is that, from a technical standpoint, some enterprise AI applications currently represent low-hanging

---

[17] David Silver, Julian Schrittwieser, Karen Simonyan, Ioannis Antonoglou, Aja Huang, Arthur Guez, Thomas Hubert, Lucas Baker, Matthew Lai, Adrian Bolton, Yutian Chen, Timothy Lillicrap, Fan Hui, Laurent Sifre, George van den Driessche, Thore Graepel, and Demis Hassabis, "Mastering the Game of Go Without Human Knowledge," *Nature*, Vol. 550, October 19, 2017.

[18] David Silver, Thomas Hubert, Julian Schrittwieser, Ioannis Antonoglou, Matthew Lai, Arthur Guez, Marc Lanctot, Laurent Sifre, Dharshan Kumaran, Thore Graepel, Timothy Lillicrap, Kern Simonyan, and Demis Hassabis, "Mastering Chess and Shogi By Self-Play with a General Reinforcement Learning Algorithm," *arXiv: 1712.01815*, 2017.

[19] AlphaStar Team, "AlphaStar: Mastering the Real-Time Strategy Game StarCraft II," webpage, 2019.

[20] Khimya Khetarpal, Zafarali Ahmed, Andre Cianflone, Riashat Islam, and Joelle Pineau, "RE-EVALUATE: Reproducibility in Evaluating Reinforcement Learning Algorithms," paper presented at the International Conference on Machine Learning, Stockholm, Sweden, 2018.

[21] See, for instance, Yann LeCun's recent ACM TechTalk (Association for Computing Machinery, "'The Power and Limits of Machine Learning' with Yann LeCun," video, YouTube, September 11, 2019).

[22] This second question considers aspects of scaling AI that are inherent to the current state of AI technology. The answer to this question provides additional guidelines against which DoD's posture for AI can be assessed in Chapter Four.

fruit for DoD, and most mission-support and especially operational AI remain further out on the horizon. Moreover, there are various challenges and risks to employing and scaling these technical advances that present differently for enterprise, mission-support, and operational AI.

Before elaborating further, we want to emphasize that by posing these questions, we are not implying that AI is just DL or DRL. On the contrary, and as we stated earlier, many technical approaches underpin AI.

Enterprise AI

In many ways, some enterprise AI applications in DoD are comparable with AI solutions currently being pursued by many organizations in the private sector and the public domain (for a sampling, see section "Industry: Advancement and Adoption" in Appendix C). Because of this, many commercial solutions exist, and their existence and relative success constitute evidence that similar technology solutions could be adopted, tailored, or specifically developed, depending on DoD's needs.

Although the technology for some enterprise AI applications currently exists and is relatively mature, that does not mean that scaling enterprise AI across organizations is devoid of obstacles and challenges (see section "Industry: Organization" in Appendix C). On the contrary, scaling AI requires periodically identifying and prioritizing investment areas for which technological solutions exist, are implementable, and would significantly improve the organization's bottom line or other critical objectives. Once these priority areas are identified, scaling AI requires making informed decisions about commercial acquisition of these solutions or developing them in-house, and it requires institutionalizing the knowledge and know-how garnered along the way. It requires ensuring the availability of the necessary infrastructure to support these solutions. In parallel, scaling up requires incentivizing potential user bases to adopt them,[23] and providing the training and reskilling required to do so. It also requires continued development of the technology, which, as many of our interviewees noted, makes AI different from traditional capabilities. Most importantly, scaling AI

---

[23] In DoD, the promise of cost savings alone might not incentivize adoption because of the opposing negative incentive effects of use it or lose it.

requires appreciating data for the critical resources they are, by systematically collecting and curating data, sharing data within the organization in support of its objectives, and strategically guarding the rights to data when commercial solutions are pursued.

Furthermore, as we noted in the previous section, the current crop of AI techniques, particularly DL approaches, rely heavily on the availability of substantial amounts of clean and tagged training data. The quality and quantity of the data available will typically influence the selection of AI approaches to solve a given problem, and the viability of applying DL techniques. More data will allow for a broader variety of potential approaches, but will also require the infrastructure to support the data's storage, governance, and processing needs. In particular, deploying enterprise AI at scale in an organization requires close cooperation with both the organizational entities in charge of data and data management (e.g., CDO) and those in charge of storage and computing infrastructure (e.g., CIO). It also requires close cooperation with the users (at many levels, from the chief analytics officer to the individual users) to ensure the most important questions are posed and answered (see the section "Industry: Advancement and Adoption" in Appendix C).

Moreover, AI tools are designed and implemented digitally, usually in software. Because of this, AI success requires success in software, though success in the latter is nowhere near sufficient to ensure success in the former.

Mission-Support AI and Operational AI

Many of the recent advances in DL that we summarized earlier, particularly those focused on classification and prediction, have important DoD applications on the horizon, especially in mission-support AI. For example, DL's recent success at object recognition in images makes intelligence, surveillance, and reconnaissance (ISR) a natural application for mission-support AI.

Yet, in spite of many promising advancements and technology demonstrations, DL algorithms remain brittle and fragile—they lack robustness, as the prevalence and diversity of adversarial examples demonstrate.[24] Moreover, they introduce new vulnerabilities and attack surfaces that demand careful consideration, ideally up front as part of the design process rather than as an afterthought.

Additionally, DL algorithms' design is currently optimized for commercial uses rather than DoD uses which manifests in various ways. For one, the performance metrics optimized for commercial applications are often misaligned with DoD needs. For example, in her December 2018 testimony to the House of Representatives' Armed Services Committee,[25] Lisa Porter, the USD(R&E), noted that commercial search applications optimize precision over recall.[26] This is one example of a technical approach that, in principle, has both commercial and DoD applications, but that, in practice, as currently implemented in the commercial world, optimizes a metric that is misaligned with the needs of the DoD application. Another example of this is that the resources involved are often misaligned with DoD needs. On this point, and going back to classifier algorithms as an example, the classifier algorithms in commercial use today need to be retrained as the data and their properties change, and the algorithms typically assume that reach-back to the cloud is available as needed for retraining. That assumption might not be valid in an operational—or perhaps even mission-support—AI application. Moreover, the large training data sets themselves might also be lacking for a battlefield environment, and the viability of using synthetic data remains to be seen.

---

[24] Christian Szegedy, Wojciech Zaremba, Ilya Sutskever, Joan Bruna, Dumitru Erhan, Ian Goodfellow, and Rob Fergus, "Intriguing Properties of Neural Networks," *arXiv: 1312.6199*, December 21, 2013.

[25] Lisa Porter, statement to the House Armed Services Committee and Subcommittee on Emerging Threats and Capabilities, "Department of Defense's Artificial Intelligence Structures, Investments, and Applications," Washington, D.C., U.S. House of Representatives, December 11, 2018.

[26] In classifier algorithms, *precision* refers to the fraction of relevant instances (true positives) among retrieved instances. *Recall* is the fraction of total relevant instances that were actually retrieved, thereby characterizing the sensitivity of the algorithm. If one is using such an algorithm to support human analysts (as is the case in Project Maven) in finding missile launchers in satellite imagery, for example, it is more important that the algorithm finds as many of the missile launchers as possible (high recall) than that the algorithm is mostly correct when it flags an object as a missile launcher (high precision).

Finally, DL techniques remain somewhat artisanal, in that they are often handcrafted for a particular application and typically do not readily generalize to others.[27] An algorithm that works well on one application might not automatically work well on another, as several of our technical interviewees emphasized (see section "Industry: Advancement and Adoption" in Appendix C).

The Critical Challenge of Validation, Verification, Testing, and Evaluation

A critical challenge across all categories of AI—one that is particularly acute in safety-critical systems employed in mission-support and operational AI—is the challenge of V&V of AI,[28] and that of its supporting counterpart of T&E.[29] V&V enables the designers of the system to trust its design, and T&E enables managers to assess whether the system meets the specified requirements and the remaining stakeholders (such as users and operators) to establish trust in it.[30]

The current state of AI VVT&E is nowhere close to ensuring the performance and safety of AI applications,[31] particularly where safety-critical systems are concerned. V&V for safety-critical control

---

[27] Transfer learning might eventually alleviate this "artisanal" issue, but it remains an area of active research at present.

[28] V&V is also widely considered in software and hardware, in simulation modeling, and in control systems, among other fields. The exact interpretation of the terms vary from field to field. The relative maturity across fields also varies.

[29] Both V&V and T&E, sometimes combined in the DoD context into the acronym VVT&E, have important implications for certification and accreditation of AI technologies and AI-enabled systems.

[30] Current DoD acquisition practices include two levels of testing and evaluation. The first is development T&E to assist in engineering design and development, and to verify that technical performance specifications have been met. The second is operational test and evaluation, to assess operational effectiveness and suitability. We are looking beyond these two levels here, to highlight difficulties in verifying, through various means, the technology during earlier stages of R&D.

[31] In the spirit of correcting common misconceptions, we strongly caution against the tendency we noted in some of our interviewees to conflate AI VVT&E with software VVT&E. The latter, itself still an open problem, particularly for software with many lines of code or software that has been repeatedly updated and added to, is only a small component of the former as we describe in our discussion.

systems is a current topic of research and usually involves either formal mathematical analysis or extensive simulations. The former, although elegant, typically lacks the ability to scale, and the latter is difficult to ground in theory to enable confidence in the result. Both also have inherent limitations in what is represented by them, and thus might miss critical elements of the real world, resulting in poor performance or errors during real world operation. V&V for ML—and for AI systems more broadly, some of which might involve interacting control and ML algorithms—is, at present, largely uncharted territory.[32] Furthermore, ML and related approaches have the additional complexity of requiring verification of training data in addition to that of the models.[33]

The idea of real-time monitoring came up in several of our interviews across industry as a practical alternative to V&V (see section "Industry: Advancement and Adoption" in Appendix C). However, the use of real-time monitoring inherently assumes that (1) one has the ability, early enough, to detect when things go wrong, (2) the consequences of that happening are manageable, and (3) taking the system offline when that happens is an option. These assumptions might not hold for DoD, particularly where mission-support and operational AI are concerned.

---

[32] V&V for ML is increasingly the focus of research interest—see, for example, DARPA's Assured Autonomy program. See Sandeep Neema, "Assured Autonomy," Defense Advanced Research Projects Agency," webpage, undated. In the spirit of correcting common misconceptions and contrary to what the nomenclature seems to imply, the *learning* in ML and DL refers to learning from data sets offline, not in real-time, as we described earlier. Lifelong learning systems that learn in real-time in response to new data remain in the distant future. See, for example, DARPA's Lifelong Learning Machines program (Hava Siegelmann, "Lifelong Learning Machines [L2M]," Defense Advanced Research Projects Agency, webpage, undated). Because of this, lifelong learning systems are not the focus of our discussion, which aims to highlight the difficulties of carrying out VVT&E for systems, even in the absence of lifelong learning.

[33] We are using the word *verification* here loosely, because it is not yet clear what this process entails for data sets. Additionally, the Partnership on AI has put out a call for public comments on its ABOUT ML project, which addresses a related need for documentation and transparency in the design of ML systems.

What Does That Mean for DoD?

Pursuing enterprise AI at scale is realistic in the near term but would require fundamentally transforming DoD's culture into a data-enabled one that values data and uses them to their full potential—a monumental endeavor but one that could enhance efficiencies across the board, in alignment with the defense objectives identified by DoD in the Summary of the 2018 NDS.[34] This is consistent with the beliefs expressed by many of our interviewees that scaling enterprise AI requires large organizational shifts and commitment from leadership rather than incremental changes. Additionally, pursuing enterprise AI at scale would help prepare DoD for adoption and scaling of mission support and operational AI as the relevant technologies mature. In sum, pursuing enterprise AI at scale would require appropriate investments in both enterprise AI use cases and applications and significant investments in infrastructure and enablers.

Deployment and use of mission support and operational AI technologies still face several significant technical barriers. We do not mean to imply that DoD should not pursue mission support or operational AI. On the contrary, we believe that it should (with particular attention paid to VVT&E, with appropriate investments made accordingly, and within ethical principles such as those proposed by the DIB). However, it is important for DoD to maintain realistic expectations for both performance and timelines in going from demonstrations of the art of the possible to deployment at scale in a DoD environment. Careful investments in mission-support and operational AI use cases need to start now, but with the expectation that they might lead to products only in the middle to long term. Moreover, these investments should be supplemented by appropriate investments in infrastructure and enablers and in VVT&E.

In view of the aforementioned, as a rough rule of thumb, the expectations for at-scale deployment of the three categories of AI,

---

[34] The *2018 Summary of the National Defense Strategy* identifies "[c]ontinuously delivering performance with affordability and speed as we change Department mindset, culture and management systems" as one of DoD's defense objectives (U.S. Department of Defense, 2018d, p. 4).

assuming adequate investments across all three categories are made starting today, can be viewed as aligned with the three time windows (near, mid, and far) described in our conceptual framework. Some enterprise AI is ready for use at scale in the near term while it is reasonably ambitious to expect new mission-support AI and operational AI to be ready for use at scale in the middle and long terms, respectively. That does not mean that specific instances of DL-based mission support or operational support capabilities will not materialize sooner— our assessment pertains to expectations of deployment at scale.[35]

It is important to emphasize here, once again, that the previous statements speak specifically to setting goals and expectations for leveraging and scaling the prominent recent advancements in AI in support of DoD's mission. It is also important to note that history has taught us that breakthroughs, particularly in AI, are hard to predict (see section "AI History in DoD" in Appendix D). For example, although the current approaches rely heavily on training on large data sets, that might not be the case in the future.[36] It is thus important for DoD to maintain agility and an open, balanced perspective as it moves further toward an AI-enabled future and a portfolio of fundamental basic research investments that could open new doors.

---

[35] For example, one can potentially conceive of more-rapid progress in operational AI for particular domains—particularly digital ones, such as electronic warfare—or uses where the consequences of failure might be less than the consequences of having no capability at all.

[36] Although the algorithms might become more efficient in using data with time, this does not negate the view of data as a critical resource to take advantage of present technological advancements.

CHAPTER FOUR

DoD Posture for Artificial Intelligence

In this chapter, we present our assessment of DoD posture in AI along each of the six dimensions we introduced in Chapter Two: organization, advancement, adoption, innovation, data, and talent. For each dimension, we begin by briefly describing what we learned from our interviews about DoD's current status and activities (detailed in Appendix B). We then highlight the obstacles and friction points that DoD is facing and that drive our recommendations in Chapter Five. For context, we begin by summarizing DoD's vision for AI and the roles of OSD entities and the services in that vision.

Context

The summary of the 2018 DoD AI Strategy presents the following vision:

> We will harness the potential of AI to transform all functions of the Department positively, thereby supporting and protecting U.S. servicemembers, safeguarding U.S. citizens, defending allies and partners, and improving the affordability, effectiveness, and speed of our operations. The women and men in the U.S. armed forces remain our enduring source of strength; we will use AI-enabled information, tools, and systems to empower, not replace, those who serve.

> Realizing this vision requires identifying appropriate use cases for AI across DoD, rapidly piloting solutions, and scaling successes

across our enterprise. The 2018 DoD AI Strategy [. . .] will drive the urgency, scale, and unity of effort needed to navigate this transformation. The Joint Artificial Intelligence Center (JAIC) is the focal point for carrying it out.[1]

The establishment of the JAIC followed the DIB's Technologies and Capabilities Recommendation 5:

Proposal: Establish a DoD center for studying artificial intelligence and machine learning and building expertise and capacity in these areas across the department. Like the institutions established in the past to ensure the DoD's technological advantage in nuclear weapons, DoD now needs a centralized, focused, well-resourced organization to propel applied research in artificial intelligence (AI) and machine learning (ML). This center should coordinate research in these areas across the Department, and liaise with other labs in the private sector and universities, and should also conduct educational efforts to inform the Department about the implications of these advances for the Defense enterprise.[2]

In particular, the JAIC was established to

accelerate the delivery of AI-enabled capabilities, scale the Department-wide impact of AI, and synchronize DoD AI activities to expand Joint Force Advantage.[3]

More specifically, the JAIC will:

Rapidly deliver AI-enabled capabilities to address key missions, strengthening current military advantages and enhancing future AI research and development efforts with mission needs, operational outcomes, user feedback, and data;

---

[1]   U.S. Department of Defense, 2018d, p. 4; U.S. Department of Defense, 2018c.

[2]   Defense Innovation Board, undated b.

[3]   U.S. Department of Defense, 2018c, p. 9.

Establish a common foundation for scaling AI's impact across DoD, leading strategic data acquisition and introducing unified data sources, reusable tools, frameworks and standards, and cloud and edge services;

Facilitate AI planning, policy, governance, ethics, safety, cybersecurity, and multilateral coordination;

Attract and cultivate a world-class AI team to supply trusted subject matter expertise on AI capability delivery and to create new accelerated learning experiences in AI across DoD at all levels of professional education and training.[4]

The memo establishing the JAIC, authored by then-DSD Patrick Shanahan, introduced a coordination role for the JAIC and clarified the role of USD(R&E):

The JAIC is intended to enhance the ability for DoD components to execute new AI initiatives, experiment, and learn within a common framework. DoD and OSD components therefore are highly encouraged to collaborate with the JAIC upon initiation of new AI initiatives. Components will initially coordinate each AI initiative that totals more than $15 million annually with the JAIC in order to ensure DoD is creating Department-wide advantages. This threshold will be reviewed annually as investments in AI mature. The JAIC Director will maintain an accounting of DoD AI initiatives as a means of synchronizing efforts and fostering collaboration. The Under Secretary of Defense for Research and Engineering will continue to promote development of new AI technologies, systems, and concepts that support AI capability delivery.[5]

An OSD directive required the armed services to develop service-specific AI strategy annexes.

---

[4] U.S. Department of Defense, 2018c, p. 9.

[5] Deputy Secretary of Defense, 2018, p. 2.

We note the sense of urgency, the breadth of scope and implications of AI, and the need for unity of effort conveyed in the aforementioned sources.

Organization

With this context in mind, we turn our attention to the organizational structures and entities with primary focus on AI in DoD. These structures and entities are nascent and in flux. This is not a criticism, but an observation—indeed, we expect these structures to continue to evolve as DoD moves toward an AI-enabled future.

At the OSD Level

When we began this study in December 2018, the JAIC had just welcomed its inaugural director, six months after it was stood up. It had a Deputy Director in place and a small staff, consisting primarily of military officers detailed from their respective services on six-month assignments. Staffing has since been expanded to 75 billets for FY 2020, and has been reorganized with a new chief science officer, a new chief technology officer, and a new chief of acquisitions, all of whom bring significant experience to their roles—experience garnered from their tenures in the technology industry, academia, and government (see section "Organization: At the OSD Level" in Appendix B). The JAIC initiated several National Mission Initiatives (NMIs) in FY 2019. These NMIs are starting use cases, per the DoD AI strategy, and include an initiative on predictive maintenance (PM) with Special Operations Command, and a second initiative on humanitarian assistance and disaster relief building on the lessons learned from Project Maven.[6] The JAIC also began work on a Joint Common Foundation (JCF), per the DoD AI strategy, focusing in particular on platforms, data pipelines, reusable tools, and standards.

---

[6] John Shanahan, "Artificial Intelligence Initiatives," statement to the Senate Armed Services Committee Subcommittee on Emerging Threats and Capabilities, Washington, D.C., U.S. Senate, March 12, 2019.

We identified the following set of impediments and friction points in organization, strategy, and resourcing at the OSD level:

DoD lacks baselines and metrics in conjunction with its AI vision. Baselines and metrics are important for two reasons. First, they are a means of assessing and enhancing progress toward DoD's vision and of managing expectations (see section "Adoption and Scaling of Unmanned Aircraft Systems" in Appendix D and section "AI History in DoD" in Appendix D). Second, metrics are needed to demonstrate value and secure continued leadership support as progress is made in institutional transformation (see section "Industry: Organization" in Appendix C); this is particularly important in ensuring continued support at the highest levels of decisionmaking, both within and outside DoD. The summary of the 2018 DoD AI strategy lays out a vision for institutional transformation through AI, the assignment of an organization to be a focal point for that transformation, and a set of activities associated with the vision. However, the strategy does not articulate baselines, metrics, or quantifiable measures of value or success.

The JAIC lacks visibility. The issue of visibility is subtle. The JAIC has been designated, in the summary of the DoD AI strategy, as the focal point for carrying out DoD's strategy, and is expected to attract and cultivate a world-class AI team. This designation and role presume a certain degree of visibility both within DoD and outside it. This visibility was lacking based on our interviews. Overall, we noted a lack of clarity among our interviewees on the JAIC's mandate, roles, and activities. We also noted a lack of clarity around how it fits within the broader DoD ecosystem and how it connects to the services and their efforts. That was true of both DoD interviewees and our industry interviewees who had heard of the JAIC (see section "Organization: At the OSD Level" in Appendix B and section "Thoughts Across Industry: On the JAIC" in Appendix C). In addition to the lack of clarity about the JAIC's current mandate and roles, there were many perspectives about the desired or ideal role for the JAIC as DoD embraces and scales AI. These perspectives ranged from the JAIC as a central repository of information and best practices, to the JAIC as a center of excellence that focuses on discrete tasks (e.g., building the JCF, formalizing standards for VVT&E), to the JAIC's potential elevation to a field agency or other entity with a direct reporting line to either the Secretary or DSD.

We do not believe this lack of clarity to be simply a question of messaging. More fundamentally, it points to a lack of clarity about the raison d'être of the JAIC and how the specific roles it has been assigned support that. The confusion might not be entirely on the part of the audience. DoD needs to have a clearer view of what it wants the JAIC to be and how DoD can help ensure the success of JAIC's mission, and therefore DoD's vision.

The DIB's Technologies and Capabilities Recommendation 5, cited earlier in this chapter, proposed establishing a centralized, focused, and well-resourced organization to propel applied research in AI and ML forward. The insights gathered from our industry interviews (see section "Industry: Organization" in Appendix C) lead us to believe there is indeed value in, if not strict necessity for, a centralized organization. This organization would have a mandate that goes beyond applied research and would be supported at the highest levels with long-term funding commitments to institute organizational change and scale AI across DoD. One of our industry interviewees noted that centralization at onset was key to their organization's success, and premature decentralization of effort likely would have been detrimental (see section "Industry: Organization" in Appendix C).[7]

Based on the premises that (1) the JAIC is the focal point of DoD AI activity; (2) it fulfills the need for a centralized, well-resourced organization to scale AI and its impact across DoD (see above); (3) it will continue in that role for several years because of the expected timeline for AI deployment at scale across enterprise, mission-support, and operational AI; and (4) it needs to be able carry out all the roles it has been tasked with in the current strategy and establishing memo, we identified friction points that we discuss in the following paragraphs.

---

[7] We note that this comment, and those of other industry interviewees, imply that if the effort to scale AI across an organization is successful, its natural ending point is the sunset of the centralized entity that drove the transformation as AI capabilities are diffused across the organization. We therefore expect the JAIC's role to evolve, though we expect that to happen along a longer timeline (ten or more years) based on our assessment of the state of technology in Chapter Three.

The JAIC lacks the authorities to carry out its present role. At its core, the JAIC's overarching mission can be distilled to this: Scale AI and its impact across DoD. This mission and its present scope—as defined by the summary of the DoD AI strategy and the memo establishing the JAIC—are extensive, while the JAIC's current authorities are limited. In particular, the JAIC is expected to synchronize DoD AI activities and coordinate AI initiatives totaling more than $15 million annually. It is unclear whether the JAIC has any mechanisms for enforcing these directives, because it does not have the authorities to direct investments or to halt programs or activities that are deemed to be misaligned with DoD's strategy (a fact we learned through multiple DoD interviews). In short, *the JAIC does not have directive or budget authorities, and that critically limits its ability to synchronize and coordinate DoD-wide AI activities to enact change.* Currently, it can catalogue these activities, but it is unclear how doing so would help scale AI across DoD. Of course, that assumes that what constitutes an AI activity is known. However, it is not currently clear how the determination of what constitutes an AI initiative or activity is made, by whom, and whether that determination is consistent across DoD.[8]

The JAIC lacks a five-year strategic road map, and a precise objective allowing it to formulate one. Our industry interviews (see section "Industry: Organization in Appendix C) and relevant literature highlight the need for five-year strategic road maps to execute organizational transformation,[9] particularly a transformation of the magnitude envisioned in the DoD AI strategy and that the JAIC has been tasked with executing. In that context, our industry interviews also emphasized the need for an objective articulated in precise-enough terms to enable the formulation of such a strategic road map (see section "Industry: Organization" in Appendix C). DoD experience with technology also highlights the importance of clearly defined, measurable goals in

---

[8] We touched upon this point earlier in Chapter Three while discussing the definition of AI. Although it is not clear that enforcing a DoD-wide definition of AI is either feasible or helpful, the question of how DoD identifies and tracks AI activities or programs remains an important open question.

[9] John M. Bryson, Lauren Hamilton Edwards, and David M. Van Slyke, "Getting Strategic About Strategic Planning Research," *Public Management Review*, Vol. 20, No. 3, 2018.

enhancing success (see section "Adoption and Scaling of Unmanned Aircraft Systems" in Appendix D). The JAIC's mission, which we have distilled to *scale AI and its impact across DoD*, is too vague to serve as a five-year objective for the purpose of this road map. The JAIC needs a refined objective that is precise, ambitious, and potentially feasible in the time frame, and that can serve to guide the development of an agile, strategic road map to include shorter-term (one-year) goals and metrics to assess progress along these goals. The existence of a five-year strategic road map would also help focus the selection of NMIs and justify their relevance to the overall objective (see "Organization: At OSD Level" in Appendix B).

The lack of longer-term budget commitments might hinder the JAIC's success. This observation is not just about the amount of funding for the JAIC—for which we have no basis to judge at present— but also the horizon, certainty (or lack thereof), and general trends of funding commitments. Our insights gleaned from industry indicate that a sizable, long-term funding commitment, generally ramping up to accompany the five-year strategic road map, is critical to ensuring success in organizational transformations to enable scaling of AI (see section "Industry: Organization" in Appendix C). Based on our inter-actions with the JAIC, we were unable to determine whether the JAIC is able to submit budget requests through the programming, planning, budgeting and execution (PPBE) system as an independent entity, allowing it to request funds for the Future Years Defense Plan (FYDP) and also allowing high-level leadership to demonstrate support for the JAIC's mission by prioritizing these budget requests.

Within the Services

The services have also all had significant activity in AI over the past year. The Army stood up an AI Task Force under the newly established AFC and established an Army AI Hub consisting of a consortium of industry, government, and academia partners based at Carnegie Mellon University (CMU).[10] The Air Force stood up an AI CFT

---

[10] See, for example, the reporting on the establishment of the Army AI hub at CMU (Matthew Nagel, "Army AI Task Force Selects Carnegie Mellon as New Hub," Carnegie Mellon

and launched the Massachusetts Institute of Technology–Air Force AI Accelerator.[11] The Navy and Marines stood up AI task forces. The Department of the Navy is also currently in the midst of a significant reorganization that will likely affect its posture for AI.[12] The Marines, as part of the Department of the Navy, are also leveraging the Navy's efforts. At the time of our interviews, neither the Navy nor the Marines had AI-specific initiatives or partnerships with universities. The Army, Air Force, and Marines developed AI strategy annexes per the OSD directive. Of these, only the Army and Air Force strategies are publicly available.[13]

We identified the following set of impediments and friction points in organization, strategy, and resourcing at the level of the individual services.

The service AI annexes lack baselines and metrics. All the (public) service annexes lack such metrics. The Army AI Strategy Annex presents an overarching strategy for the Army,[14] decomposed in terms of *ends* (goals of the strategy), *ways* (underlying methods and an initial set of projects), and *means* (the manner in which the strategy will be implemented).[15] The strategy mentions a forthcoming integration plan with more detail on organization, methods, and implementation, but the present strategy does not present metrics or quantifiable measures to assess progress toward the ends. Likewise, the Air Force AI

University, blog post, December 4, 2018).

[11] See, for instance, the reporting on the establishment of the MIT-Air Force AI Accelerator hub (Rob Matheson, "MIT and U.S. Air Force Sign Agreement to Launch AI Accelerator," *MIT News*, blog post, May 20, 2019).

[12] We heard of plans to set up a Navy AI Task Force but were unable to confirm its existence at the time of the report.

[13] Under Secretary of the Army, "Army Artificial Intelligence Strategy Annex Submission," memorandum for Chief Information Office, Office of the Secretary of Defense, Washington, D.C.: U.S. Department of Defense, 2019; U.S. Department of the Air Force, *The United States Air Force Artificial Intelligence Annex to the Department of Defense Artificial Intelligence Strategy*, Washington, D.C., 2019.

[14] Although not exclusively focused on operational AI and mission-support AI, the Army AI strategy seems to emphasize those over enterprise AI.

[15] Under Secretary of the Army, 2019; U.S. Department of the Air Force, 2019.

strategy annex defines five focus areas and associated sets of activities,[16] but does not propose metrics or quantifiable measures to assess progress toward these lines of effort.[17] We note here the high divergence between the Army and the Air Force AI strategies, which indicate that these two services are moving in very different directions. In particular, the Army AI strategy annex focuses primarily on operational AI capabilities, while the Air Force annex focuses on establishing the foundations and infrastructure needed to enable AI.

When mandates and authorities of the service AI organizations exist, they appear to be limited. Based on our interviews, the role and mandate of the Army AI Task Force appear to be modeled after that of the JAIC. However, that is difficult to ascertain because the Army AI strategy annex does not clearly enunciate a mandate and role for the Army AI Task Force as the DoD AI strategy does for the JAIC. Regardless, the extent and sufficiency of the Army AI Task Force's authorities (directive, budgetary, or otherwise), appear to be limited (see section "Organization: Within the Services" in Appendix B).

The Air Force AI CFT, co-led by an Air Force captain, appears to function as a tiger team more than anything else. One of its tasks was to facilitate the standing up of the MIT–Air Force AI Accelerator. Further roles, goals, or mandates are unclear, though the signaling, specifically the choice of a captain to co-lead it, indicates that this is not a significant effort to centralize (see section "Organization: Within the Services" in Appendix B).

The authorities of the Navy's AI Task Force and that of the Marine's AI Task Force remain unclear to us based on our interviews (see section "Organization: Within the Services" in Appendix B).

---

[16] These areas are

(1) drive down technology barriers to entry; (2) recognize and treat data as a strategic asset; (3) democratize access to artificial intelligence solutions; (4) recruit, develop, upskill, and cultivate our workforce; and (5) increase transparency and cooperation with international, government, industry, and academic partners.

[17] Under Secretary of the Army, 2019; U.S. Department of the Air Force, 2019.

Advancement and Adoption

Our starting point at the onset of our study was the DoD model of technology development, procurement, fielding, and sustainment, giving rise to two dimensions of posture assessment related to technologies: advancement and adoption. However, as we carried out our study, it became clear that this model is not valid for AI, owing to the spiral nature of AI technology development. This spiral process consists of the iterative design (including training) and deployment of the systems. Moreover, the operators are, ideally, intimately involved in this process and give continual feedback to the developers at all stages of development. Because of the spiral nature of AI technology development, we have opted to combine these two dimensions in our presentation of findings throughout our report (here, in Chapter Five, and in Appendixes B and C).

Our team interviewed staff from DARPA and the service labs (AFRL, ARL, NRL, and the Marine Corps Warfighting Laboratory) to better understand DoD's R&D activities and environment, and the enablers and obstacles therein. Those entities both drive DoD R&D and stimulate activity in industry to meet at least nearer-term demand. Our team also met with acquisition executives across the services and within OSD, and with potential AI users and operators covering the range of enterprise, mission-support, and operational AI.

Because it is difficult to predict which technological advances will pan out (see section "The Offset Strategy" in Appendix D), the research organizations are thinking broadly about the future beyond incremental advances to develop robust AI and explainable AI, seek fundamental algorithmic advances to drive the next generation of AI advances, better understand the human-AI interaction to enhance the development of AI systems,[18] and develop the foundations for V&V of AI systems. As we noted in Chapter Three, our interviewees agreed that V&V of AI systems is a critical topic that DoD will need to address, particularly when it seeks to deploy and use safety-critical AI systems.

---

[18] Interviewees both inside and outside DoD emphasized the importance of improving the understanding of human-machine interaction.

However, like our academic and industry interviewees (see section "Industry: Advancement and Adoption" in Appendix C), the interviewees lacked current V&V solutions and could not predict which technical avenues toward V&V would eventually prove to be effective for AI systems. Concerns about the "valley of death" and the failures in transitioning research to prototypes and products, both broadly and specifically for AI, also came up in our interviews.[19] Finally, although our interviewees generally agreed that AI will have a bigger role to play, they also emphasized the need for training and experimentation to build trust and enhance adoption of these technologies, while noting that generational factors might help down the line.[20]

Beyond the technology assessment, including challenges and risks we described in Chapter Three, we identified the following impediments and friction points about technology advancement and adoption.

The extent to which DoD acquisition pathways support AI development remains unclear. The DIB's SWAP study findings highlighted the incompatibility between the current "development, procurement, sustainment" model with software, and recommended the development of new acquisition pathways for software.[21] DoD recently implemented an Adaptive Acquisition Framework, consisting of several potential acquisition approaches.[22] This framework allows the acquisition strategy to be aligned with the acquisition approach most appropriate for the technology. As noted in our review of the state of AI (Chapter Three) and in our industry interviews (see section "Academia: Advancement and Adoption" in Appendix C, and "Industry: Advancement and Adoption" in Appendix C), the development of AI systems is spiral rather than linear, consisting of the iterative design (including training) and deployment of AI systems. Moreover, once fielded, the systems need to be retrained to maintain performance, potentially

---

[19] The term *valley of death* refers to the failure of promising research projects to transition into specific products or capabilities.

[20] The term *generational factors* refers to younger personnel who might generally be more comfortable with digital technologies.

[21] Defense Innovation Board, 2019b.

[22] Defense Acquisition University, "Digital Acquisition Prototypes," webpage, undated.

every few days or even every few hours. Because of this spiral development process, the most appropriate pathway within the new Adaptive Acquisition Framework would appear to be that of software acquisition (even as we emphasize, again, that AI is not software). This pathway consists of an initial planning phase, followed by a series of iterative spirals to reach a minimum viable product then minimum viable capability release. The pathway continues to cycle through spirals to final release. Whether this pathway provides a viable path forward for AI remains to be tested and assessed. Regardless, beyond the structure of the development and acquisition model, the length of acquisition processes often pose potential hurdles for technologies with fast development and deployment cycles.[23] Whether these concerns will be alleviated within the new framework also remains to be seen.

Communication channels among the builders—and users— of AI within DoD are sparse. For example, one of the takeaways from our interviews is that communication among the research organizations appears to be limited, and when it does occur, it is driven primarily by personal connections among program managers or researchers (see section "Advancement and Adoption" in Appendix B). This sparsity of communication is inconsistent with the culture of openness and sharing that was emphasized by our academic and industry interviewees as a driver of success (see section "Industry: Innovation" in Appendix C, and section "Academia: Advancement and Adoption" in Appendix C).[24] Likewise, we noted AI RDT&E activities throughout the services, but our takeaway from the interviews was that visibility into these activities is limited, both within and across the services and from OSD. Finally, mechanisms of interactions between the developers

---

[23] Isaac R. Porche, III, Shawn McKay, Megan McKernan, Robert Warren Button, Bob Murphy, Katheryn Giglio, and Elliot Axelband, *Rapid Acquisition and Fielding for Information Assurance and Cyber Security in the Navy*, Santa Monica, Calif.: RAND Corporation, TR-1294-NAVY, 2012.

[24] We should emphasize here that the sparsity of communication appeared to be driven by the lack of formalized communication channels rather than an unwillingness to communicate.

(e.g., research entities) and users (e.g., warfighters, analytics officers) of AI are limited or nonexistent.[25]

There are many potential impediments to users adopting AI technologies. Those include an inherent resistance to change—including in roles and TTPs; concerns about the potential loss of an individual's value to the organization as a result of the adoption of AI capabilities; and lacking trust in the technologies.[26] These perceived impediments are not unique to DoD; our interviews in industry and academia highlighted similar concerns (Appendix C). Nonetheless, these are serious concerns, and ones that DoD needs to address to effectively scale AI.

There is a lack of consensus on the delineation of AI investments within DoD. This finding points to a set of practical questions that DoD needs to answer: For the purpose of accounting for AI investments, what counts as an AI activity and what does not? As is also the case with software, DoD budgets do not account for AI when it is a small part of a larger platform, making it hard to track overall spending on AI. We note here that adopting a DoD-wide definition of AI does not necessarily provide an answer to these practical problems.[27]

Innovation

Although traditional DoD prime contractors might be broadening and deepening their AI capacity, they are doing so against a backdrop of commercial company progress in developing and implementing AI. We interviewed the service labs and DARPA (in their roles as internal innovators) and the DIU and the NSIN (in their roles of bringing external innovation into DoD) by focusing on rapid development and

---

[25] We note here that the services appeared to have recognized this friction point, as it came up in our interviews.

[26] The lack of trust in the technologies is a valid concern, in view of the fragility of these approaches and the lack of V&V foundations and practices (see Chapter Three).

[27] We previously discussed the difficulties and potential pitfalls of defining AI (see Chapter Three).

demonstration of working prototypes of new technologies or innovative uses of existing technologies.[28] Although some of these organizations are too young to fully assess their progress toward increasing DoD contracting with nontraditional firms, interviewees indicated that early data show promise toward meeting this objective, but some obstacles remain in place. More importantly, these organizations value metrics and are beginning to use them to assess their own progress toward their individual goals.[29]

However, it would be constraining to equate all innovation with *technological* innovation, as innovation can happen in many ways, including innovative uses of existing technologies, organizational and process innovation, and innovation in acquisition. Because of this, we also carried out interviews at the SCO, focusing on innovative adaptation of existing technologies to meet the needs of warfighters, and inquired about innovation in some of our interviews outside the above-mentioned organizations.

We were able to identify the following obstacles, which are not AI-specific, but nonetheless affect DoD's ability to scale AI.

Innovation within DoD might be hampered by current practices and processes or their implementation. The typical short-term duration of research projects and the lack of flexible funding allowing researchers at the service labs to pursue research projects of interest are both perceived by interviewees as hampering innovation within DoD. Moreover, DoD's hierarchical structure runs contrary to the practice of empowering employees at the lowest levels in an organization to enhance innovation, as highlighted in our industry interviews (see sec-

---

[28] NSIN was established as an experimental organization named MD5 in October 2016, and has since been renamed NSIN and moved under DIU. Many other organizations—including AFWERX, SOFWERX, AFC, and others—have similar roles promoting external innovation solutions. We had to make decisions on what to prioritize in terms of interviews, in light of the time sensitivity of this study.

[29] We heard about metrics from different organizations. For example, NSIN has recently adopted five key performance indicators, and DIU has an established set of five metrics. These are positive signs. However, these local metrics, and others like them, do not negate the need for DoD to develop a set of metrics associated with its vision of transforming DoD through AI at scale.

tion "Industry: Innovation" in Appendix C). Apparent confusion over which appropriation (e.g., RDT&E 6.1, 6.2) should be used for AI research presents added difficulties, even when support and a funding source are identified. Finally, a lack of data access and a lack of ability to share data were both cited as concerns and inhibitors to innovation, which is not surprising, given academia and industry's emphases on sharing and data as means of promoting innovation (see section "Industry: Innovation" in Appendix C, and section "Academia: Data" in Appendix C).

Current practices and processes also inhibit the ability to bring in external innovation. Although the existing acquisition pathways provide flexibilities to tailor the acquisition process, in practice, they often involve lengthy cycles and complex processes that require significant efforts and drive up costs. Those circumstances could place undue burdens on startups,[30] although DoD acquires major programs through larger prime contractors. A RAND study on cyber acquisition, although not specific to startups, highlighted many similar concerns.[31] OSD and the services have created several entities in recent years that function outside the traditional procurement process and serve as the focal point for startup engagement (e.g., NSIN, DIU, AFWERX, SOFWERX, NavalX). There has also been some evidence of success in rapid acquisition by agile, focused organizations that coordinate with diverse organizations within and outside DoD (see section "Big Safari" in Appendix D). Finally, Other Transaction Authority provides more-flexible contracting for certain prototype and production projects. Nonetheless, the consensus among our interviewees appeared to be that problems persist: DoD continues to struggle to successfully contract with startups and to attract innovators and researchers to engage with DoD. Another point raised by our interviewees in the defense industrial base were the difficulties in securing access to DoD data, thereby hampering innovation (see section "Industry: Innovation" in Appendix C). The counterpart to that, of course,

---

[30] Geoff Orazem, Greg Mallory, Matthew Schlueter, and Danny Werfel, "Why Startups Don't Bid on Government Contracts," Boston Consulting Group, webpage, August 22, 2017.

[31] Porche et al., 2012.

are the concerns about data ownership, which we return to in the next section.

Another factor potentially interfering with external innovation in DoD was raised by some of our interviewees, who mused that the public perception of DoD and its uses of AI might dampen the enthusiasm of some companies and external innovators to work with DoD (see section "Innovation" in Appendix B).

Data

The study team interviewed and collected input from many DoD stakeholders with responsibility for data and infrastructure. The team also interviewed DoD personnel who use these data and infrastructure for analytics or AI purposes. One striking aspect of our interviews was the general enthusiasm expressed for the JCF, with "wish lists" that included the development of uniform policies for sandboxing and application programming interfaces,[32] the development of common algorithm libraries and repositories for open source projects, and reuse of code components and documentation of best practices (see section "Organization: At the OSD Level" in Appendix B).

A notable development within DoD is the recent creation of the CDO role, with Michael Conlin in place as DoD's first CDO as of August 2018. We anticipate that with time, the data posture of DoD will significantly evolve. Nonetheless, through our interviews, we identified several serious obstacles and impediments in regard to data at present.

Data are not collected and stored at every opportunity. DoD's software infrastructure exists in an environment in which storage space remains a scarce resource and many opportunities to record data are missed. Even if modern storage infrastructure capacities were acquired, additional barriers might prevent the mass collection and storage of

---

[32] *Sandboxing* refers to providing an isolated environment for experimentation with software. Sandbox environments would ideally have some amount of test data and computing resources but are set up so that what happens in the sandbox is isolated from the production environment that supports actual real-world operations.

data. In particular, DoD still faces significant constraints on network bandwidth, which can hamper the ability to move data collected from sensors in the field to a location where they can be stored. Additionally, DoD's suite of software was designed for and implemented in an era in which applications stored only data for which DoD had an immediate use, rather than speculatively storing data that could be mined for insights by professionals. This situation has resulted both in inadequate data storage and in storage of less-appropriate data; in addition, too much of the data collected have already been transformed from a raw, foundational form into an intermediate or aggregated result. These transformations, although an appropriate optimization at the time, strip away crucial context from information needed to train modern ML-based algorithms. Finally, outdated collection processes result in some data not being collected and digitized; recent RAND work on acquisition data within DoD illustrates this point.[33]

Access to existing data is limited. Several barriers within DoD present substantial obstacles to data-sharing today. First, personnel might view data as a means of retaining power or value in DoD or of protecting their work from extensive oversight, and therefore those personnel resist data-sharing. Additionally, many data owners resist sharing their data out of security concerns and the worry that another organization might suffer a security breach. Finally, the security clearance process and other bureaucratic procedures can introduce a significant lag before an individual will be allowed to access data. This problem presents a particular difficulty in recruiting new talent into DoD, and substantially lowers productivity, even for long-standing DoD personnel. Some of these issues, as they pertain to acquisition data, were highlighted in a recent RAND report.[34] Informal networks can sub-

---

[33] Jeffrey A. Drezner, Megan McKernan, Austin Lewis, Ken Munson, Devon Hill, Jaime L. Hastings, Geoffrey McGovern, Marek N. Posard, and Jerry M. Sollinger, *Issues with Access to Acquisition Data and Information in the Department of Defense: Identification and Characterization of Data for Acquisition Category (ACAT) II–IV, Pre-MDAPs, and Defense Business Systems*, Santa Monica, Calif.: RAND Corporation, March 2019, Not available to the general public.

[34] Philip S. Anton, Megan McKernan, Ken Munson, James G. Kallimani, Alexis Levedahl, Irv Blickstein, Jeffrey A. Drezner, and Sydne Newberry, *Assessing the Use of Data*

stantially reduce the delay in gaining access to data, but based on our interviews, these workarounds appear to be haphazard.

Lack of interoperability in systems across DoD creates challenges. Interoperability of data collected by different systems, even within the same functional domain, remains a problem. Software applications within DoD have not typically been designed to work with other DoD applications—even applications in the same functional domain. Consequently, establishing relationships between data collected by one system and data collected by another can be virtually impossible. Even worse, it appears that DoD leadership is often presented with inconsistent values originating from different systems for the same data point, undermining leadership's willingness to trust data from DoD systems or make decisions based on data at all (see section "Data" in Appendix B).

The data that exist are not always understandable or traceable. DoD systems frequently lack the documentation or metadata required to provide context as to what particular data actually mean or how they were generated. For example, an Army database might store a numeric value for the number of tanks at a particular facility, but it might not explain whether this number indicates all functional tanks, all tanks assigned to a particular unit, or all tanks of any status present at the location. Other data values with less descriptive names will frequently be even more difficult to comprehend and use. The lack of any centralized tool for data service means that it is difficult for DoD personnel, even in leadership, to discover what data might be available to inform a question. Instead, discovering new data sources and interpreting them typically requires personal networks or other informal mechanisms.

In sum, all indications are that DoD data are not currently being used to their full potential. Overall, the problems we noted here represent a formidable obstacle to implementing AI algorithms,[35] even at the level of enterprise AI. Both Project Maven and the JAIC's preventa-

---

Analytics in Department of Defense Acquisition, Santa Monica, Calif.: RAND Corporation, RB-10085-OSD, 2019.

[35] Also highlighted in the DIB SWAP study (Defense Innovation Board, 2019b).

tive maintenance prototype have found that issues around data quality and availability are a primary barrier to progress (see section "Data" in Appendix B). These issues, if left unresolved, will continue to hamper the development and deployment of AI throughout DoD. Additionally, we highlight the following friction point.

There is ambiguity in data ownership where external vendors are involved. In theory, data that originate in DoD should be owned by DoD. In practice, when DoD data are analyzed or otherwise worked on by external vendors, the ownership of the data, albeit in a new modified form, becomes murky. This issue was highlighted in recent unpublished RAND work addressing weapon system intellectual property and data rights. This ambiguity of ownership leads to multiple problems beyond the specific ownership and potential loss of control of the data, including vendor lock to retain use of the data, the inability to aggregate data across multiple vendors, and the inability to use the data for additional internal purposes, among others. Although this problem is not unique to DoD, as some of our industry interviewees described (see section "Industry: Data" in Appendix C), it is one that DoD also needs to come to terms with.

Talent

To better understand how DoD is thinking about its AI talent needs, the study team met with DoD staff with primary responsibility for the hiring and management of civilian and military personnel in OSD and across the services. On the positive side, the services are actively leveraging their hiring flexibilities, both for civilians and the officer corps. For example, multiple interviewees noted that they expect that the new Cyber Excepted Service hiring authority and changes to the Defense Officers Personnel Management Act will be valuable for recruiting AI talent.

Interviewees also discussed approaches to identifying both new and existing technical talent, although most of these discussions were not specific to AI. Internally, the services are in the process of implementing various repositories for uniformed servicemembers to voluntarily register their technical capabilities.[36] Externally, identifying technical talent is less formalized, though some formal means of attracting technical talent through graduate fellowships and lab-hosted annual competitions were mentioned. Interviewees commonly noted that, like their industry counterparts (see section "Industry: Talent" in Appendix C), they find civilian talent from informal networks and contacts, particularly for the research labs, who leveraged longstanding contacts in academia and industry to access talent.

Nonetheless, through our interviews, we identified the following impediments.

DoD lacks clear mechanisms for defining and tracking AI talent. This situation is because of the lack of an AI workforce classification and the lack of consensus on the definition and requisite skills of an AI worker. Currently, the technical AI talent that exists is being placed inconsistently in military and civilian occupational specialties. For example, our interviewees across the services noted that civilian AI talent is found across occupations, including operations researchers, program analysts, scientists, software developers, and engineers. On the uniformed side, the Army and Navy are actively considering a new occupational specialty for servicemembers just for AI, but the Air Force and Marines are not. Adding to this complicated picture, some existing uniformed and civilian occupations that might have a role to play in developing AI technologies, such as software engineers, are classified as cyber talent (see section "DoD Posture for Cyber" in Appendix D). On this note, although it is not prevalent, we observed an inclination among some of our interviewees to view AI, software, cyber, and data science as somewhat interchangeable, particularly with regard to technical talent.[37]

---

[36] For example, the Army has a new marketplace that will play a role in officer assignments, and the Air Force now makes note of applicants' scores on computer language aptitude proficiency tests.

[37] Although cyber might currently offer a pathway for hiring technical AI talent, as we mentioned earlier, there also appeared to be a belief that one could readily use or otherwise retrain cyber talent, including software engineers, as technical AI talent. Even though some industry interviewees indicated existing efforts to retrain their software engineers to become

DoD struggles to grow and cultivate AI talent. Our interviews suggest a mixed appreciation for what technical AI talent consists of and which AI talent is needed. Several entities we interviewed, such as the service labs, had a clear sense of AI talent needs, but the majority were still in the beginning stages of such considerations and were more likely to emphasize contracting out for technical talent. Moreover, for those that were clear on AI talent needs, it was a challenge to define the exact knowledge, skills, and abilities they perceived that were required. Ultimately, the AI talent needs of DoD (type,[38] quantity, and mix) will depend on the broader strategy pursued for scaling AI, and the extent to which scaling AI will rely on the development of products in-house as opposed to through contracting and outsourcing. The skill sets needed for development of products in-house are significantly different from those needed for contracting and outsourcing, though all AI talent (technical or managerial) is difficult to access in the present market. Nonetheless, the consensus is that DoD faces stiff competition for AI skills and expertise, as evidenced by our interviews across academia, industry, and DoD.[39] Many of our DoD interviewees discussed the challenges related to attracting and recruiting technical talent more generally, and expressed the belief that AI talent would be no different. In that spirit, we point to a recent RAND study on career paths for data scientists within the Defense Intelligence Agency.[40] Interviews across DoD cited intense competition with the private sector, the limited ability to compete on salary, and long hiring processes. At the same

---

ML developers (see section "Industry: Talent" in Appendix C), that approach will not lead to the development of ML experts.

[38] Our industry interviews highlighted four types of AI talent: experts, ML developers, application developers, and project or program managers (see section "Industry: Talent" in Appendix C).

[39] Reasons for such stiff competition include salaries and inability to hire at competitive speed. Our interviewees had thoughts on how DoD might better compete (see section "Talent" in Appendix B, section "Industry: Talent" in Appendix C, and section "Academia: Talent" in Appendix C).

[40] Bradley Knopp, Sina Beaghley, Aaron Frank, Rebeca Orrie, and Michael Watson, *Defining the Roles, Responsibilities, and Functions for Data Science Within the Defense Intelligence Agency*, Santa Monica, Calif.: RAND Corporation, RR-1582-DIA, 2016.

time, the majority of our interviewees were optimistic that DoD could compete well on mission and the opportunity to work on important and interesting problems (see section "Talent" in Appendix B, and section "Thoughts Across Industry: On DoD Competing for AI Talent" in Appendix C).[41]

We note that similar themes to the ones we highlight here appear in the DIB's SWAP study, even as we reemphasize that AI is not software.[42]

Overall, the services generally acknowledged the need for greater permeability of technical talent between civilians and uniformed services.[43] Several interviewees expressed the belief that they need to exploit existing authorities for civilians to do a tour of duty for several years at DoD, with one noting they would be more than happy to take technical talent that was "burned out" in industry or academic jobs and wanted a change. This idea complements what we heard from industry and academia, where a variety of mechanisms are used to support external activity of employees in the interests of retaining them (see section "Academia: Talent" in Appendix C, and section "Industry: Talent" in Appendix C). Interviewees also described retention efforts for current service members with technical skills; these efforts leverage existing programs that enable some degree of permeability. This process includes formal training and rotation opportunities for officers in technical disciplines through established partnerships with indus-

---

[41] In this context, the Defense Digital Service was brought up as an example of how it is possible to still attract top talent, even with lower pay.

[42] Defense Innovation Board, 2019b.

[43] We use *permeability* to refer to the ability of personnel to move readily among reserve, active duty, and civilian roles within DoD, and various roles outside DoD in academia or industry, within a meaningful career trajectory that builds on and rewards previous experience.

try and academia.[44] A recent congressionally mandated RAND study catalogues more examples of such rotation programs.[45]

Regardless of the approach taken, if DoD is to be successful in scaling AI, it needs to ensure it has access to some level of AI talent, both technical (R&D) and managerial (acquisition), and that the talent that exists maintains its knowledge and skills in a fast-changing technical environment. DoD also needs to cultivate respect of and promotions for military personnel involved in AI activities and to compete in an AI talent market in which individuals expect change (in jobs and employers) every few years.

Overall Assessment

Although we see some positive signs, our assessment is that DoD's posture in AI is significantly challenged across all dimensions of our posture assessment.

---

[44] For example, the Air Force has internal opportunities for officers with technical skills to rotate to industry-partnered programs, such as Kessel Run. The Navy has its Fleet Scholar Education Program with CMU, while the Air Force has its Air Force Education with Industry Fellowship.

[45] Laura Werber, John A. Ausink, Lindsay Daugherty, Brian M. Phillips, Felix Knutson, and Ryan Haberman, *An Assessment of Gaps in Business Acumen and Knowledge of Industry Within the Defense Acquisition Workforce*, Santa Monica, Calif.: RAND Corporation, RR-2825-OSD, 2019.

CHAPTER FIVE

Recommendations

We conclude our report with a set of recommendations for DoD. Although the recommendations are broadly aligned with the dimensions of this posture assessment, we have additionally opted to organize them into *strategic recommendations*—those requiring a significant effort or major institutional shift—and *tactical recommendations*—those detailing more-localized actions in support of the strategic recommendations or otherwise contributing to enhancing DoD's posture. Overall, we have four strategic recommendations and seven tactical ones. We present the strategic recommendations first, highlighting the tactical recommendations as they support the strategic ones. Strategic recommendations are marked "S," and tactical ones are marked "T."

Organization

We begin by revisiting DoD's vision for AI and the means of achieving that vision. As we noted in Chapter Four, there is a lack of clarity about the raison d'être of the JAIC, and how the specific mandate and roles it has been assigned—and the visibility and authorities it has been given—support that. DoD needs to be consistent in its intent, actions, and messaging. Our first strategic recommendation therefore addresses DoD's vision for AI and the governance structures that would support this vision, as articulated in the DoD AI strategy.

Recommendation S-1: DoD should adapt AI governance structures that align authorities and resources with the mission of scaling AI.

As we noted in Chapter Four, DoD's vision for AI and the scale, urgency, and unity of efforts conveyed in that vision are at odds with the visibility, authorities, and resources it has provided to the JAIC—the focal point of DoD AI. DoD needs to develop governance and organizational structures that align authorities and resources with its vision of scaling AI across DoD.

The insights gathered from our industry interviews and the supporting change management literature (see section "Industry: Organization" in Appendix C) lead us to believe there is value in, if not strict necessity of, a centralized effort supported at the highest levels with long-term funding commitments to institute organizational change and scale AI across DoD. Indeed, one of our industry interviewees even noted that centralization at onset was key to their organization's success, and premature decentralization of effort would have likely been detrimental (see section "Industry: Organization" in Appendix C).[1]

Starting from that premise, we highlight two possible options for organizational and governance structures, and the rationale for them, although noting that other options might be viable as well, subject to further study. The first option would likely require congressional support to execute, while the second can be executed without, as it aligns with current DoD procedures and organizational structures.

Option 1: *Enhance the visibility and authorities of the JAIC to enable it to carry out its mission of scaling AI and its impact across DoD, including budgetary and workforce authorities over the military services.*

Option 2: *Take a two-pronged organizational approach as follows:*

- *Establish a JAIC council chaired by the JAIC director and consisting of one AI leadership representative from each service.*[2]

---

[1]   We note that this comment, and those of other industry interviewees, imply that if the effort to scale AI across an organization is successful, its natural ending point might be the sunset of the centralized entity that drove the transformation as AI capabilities are diffused across the organization. We therefore expect the JAIC's role to evolve, though we expect that to happen along a longer timeline (ten or more years), based on our assessment of the state of AI technologies in Chapter Three.

[2]   Regardless of which governance structure is instituted, if any, establishment of a JAIC council, as described, could facilitate coordination between the JAIC and the services.

- *Establish or reinforce a centralized AI coordination and investment organization within each of the services, with appropriate visibility and authorities, to facilitate scaling AI and its impact across the service, and to promote mandated coordination with the JAIC.*

In either option:
- *The DSD should provide the JAIC director with opportunities, at least annually, to present and be heard at the Deputy's Management Action Group (DMAG) forum (or whichever Deputy Secretary–level forum performs the functions of the DMAG).*[3]

The rationale for Option 1 is as follows: There is evidence to support that DoD has taken the right approach in establishing the JAIC as a centralized focal point for DoD's AI strategy (see Chapter 4, Organization). The evidence also suggests that the JAIC, pending initial success, will need to continue in that role for several years because of the expected timeline for AI deployment across enterprise, mission-support, and operational AI (Chapter Three). What DoD needs to do now is continue on that path by providing the requisite high-level support, visibility, and authorities (including directive and budget authorities) to enable the JAIC to enact change. Doing so would ensure that the JAIC has a chance of succeeding at its mandate of scaling AI and its impact across DoD. It would also ensure that DoD's intent, messaging, and actions are all consistent.

Having said that, we recognize that this option runs counter to DoD history and precedents, particularly because of the recent reform leading to the dissolution of the USD for Acquisition, Technology, and Logistics, and subsequent creation of the USD(R&E) and USD(A&S)

---

[3] The DMAG is the primary civilian-military management forum that supports the Secretary of Defense and addresses top DoD issues that have resource, management, and broad strategic and/or policy implications. The DMAG's primary mission is to produce advice for the DSD in a collaborative environment and to ensure that the DMAG execution aligns with the Secretary of Defense's priorities and the planning and programming schedule. The DMAG is cochaired by the DSD and Vice Chairman of the Joint Chiefs of Staff, with secretaries of the military departments, chiefs of the military services, and DoD principal staff assistants holding standing invitations. See U.S. Department of Defense, Chief Management Officer, "Deputy's Management Action Group (DMAG)," webpage, undated.

that took effect in February 2018. By enacting this reform, Congress intentionally weakened the directive authorities that OSD principals had over the services, and devolved significant procurement and acquisition authorities back to the services. We also recognize that it might not be entirely appropriate to compare DoD with a large company but rather to a large conglomerate because of the historical role and independence of the services. Therefore, we offer an alternative construct that would work within the present system to provide some level of centralization within OSD and within each of the individual services, and to provide clear mechanisms for the JAIC to work with the services and DoD leadership.

Indeed, taking the two-pronged approach laid out in Option 2 would ensure that there is some requisite level of centralization at both the OSD and service levels, taking the insights gleaned from industry regarding the necessity of such centralization for organizational transformation and the scaling of AI (see section "Industry: Organization" in Appendix C). This approach would also provide a reasonable mechanism—within the current systems and processes—for the JAIC to carry out its coordination role. This mechanism would rely on the directive authorities of the DSD to enact necessary change and resource allocations and would provide a venue for the JAIC to make the case for the use of these authorities, as needed, through at least annual DMAG engagements. Such DMAG engagements would provide an opportunity for leadership of the key AI service organizations to have seats at the table when the JAIC director presents to the DMAG, and would enable discussion and adjudication—at the highest level within the JAIC—of the JAIC's proposals and recommendations. The JAIC council would provide a meaningful and regular mechanism for the JAIC to engage with AI leadership within the services for coordination and information exchange.

The mission of scaling AI across DoD does seem to require centralizing authority consistent with one of these two options. However, given the practical realities of implementing these options at DoD, we acknowledge that DoD might be able to make meaningful, if slower, progress by anchoring the JAIC's role with more-modest but essential missions, such as setting policy and standards and developing centers of excellence and best practices. Centralizing such functions is likely a necessary part of scaling AI, but it is unlikely to be sufficient to make rapid and meaningful progress across DoD. An examination of other governance models would be a subject of further study.

Regardless of which option, if any, is followed for Recommendation S-1, Recommendations T-1, T-3, and T-4 outline the steps that the JAIC needs to take to have some chance of succeeding at its mission. Should the services follow our recommendation of setting up or reinforcing centralized AI organizations with clear mandates and with the appropriate visibility and authorities to match their mandates, Recommendation T-2 outlines the steps these organizations similarly need to take to ensure some chance of succeeding at their respective missions.

Recommendation T-1: The JAIC should develop a five-year strategic road map—backed by baselines and metrics and expected to be the first of several to follow—to execute the mission of scaling AI and its impact.

Best practices highlight the need for agile five-year strategic plans or road maps to guide institutional transformations (see section "Industry: Organization" in Appendix C).[4] Moreover, typical failure modes highlighted in our industry interviews include the lack of vision and the launch of multiple isolated pet projects that do not connect to a clear vision (see section "Industry: Organization" in Appendix C). Our insights from industry and case studies (see section "History of AI in DoD" in Appendix D and section "Adoption and Scaling of Unmanned Aircraft Systems" in Appendix D) highlight the importance of metrics to enabling success. Ideally, these metrics would be readily relatable to the overall objective and to the bottom line of the organization.

The JAIC's broad mission statement (scaling AI and its impact) does not provide a sufficiently precise objective to allow for the development of such a strategic road map. Moreover, scaling AI across DoD is anticipated to be a longer-term endeavor because of the breadth of AI in

---

[4] In reference to our use of the term *agile*, although the objective is precise, clear, and fixed, the path toward it is not and might need to vary, depending on technology or other developments.

DoD (enterprise, mission-support, and operational AI) and the current state and limitations of the technology, particularly in mission-support and operational AI (see Chapter Three). Because of this, we anticipate a sequence of five-year strategic plans ultimately will be required to achieve DoD's vision of harnessing the potential of AI to its full extent, as mission-support and operational AI mature to allow use at scale.[5] However, the starting point is now, and it requires the development of the first five-year strategic road map with an eye toward what might follow. We recommend that the JAIC develop a five-year strategic plan that is aligned with the overarching goal of scaling AI across DoD and is built around a precisely articulated objective that is ambitious and realistic, enabling it to make significant and enduring progress. Consistent with our analysis in Chapter Three, we recommend that the JAIC focus on the objective of scaling enterprise AI across DoD while establishing the foundational enablers and cultural shift required to prepare DoD for an AI-enabled future across the spectrum of uses. Although this appears to be a less exciting objective than scaling operational AI, it is an objective with a greater chance of success because of the current state of technology, it paves the way for success in scaling operational AI in the future, and it is consistent with one of the defense objectives articulated in the summary of the 2018 DoD National Defense Strategy: "Continuously delivering performance with speed as we change Departmental mindset, culture and management systems."[6] This plan should remain agile in its execution to allow for swift course correction and should be broken down into one-year short-term goals that would help drive the formulation of metrics and provide quick wins and a demonstration of value. This would also ensure that the NMIs, when selected in alignment with the objective, achieve their full potential to enable transformation at scale rather than being a collection of individual projects. It would also guide the submission of budget requests

---

[5]   The inherent assumption here is that the JAIC has been successful in its initial five-year road map. A review of the JAIC's performance and progress might be in order at that juncture.

[6]   U.S. Department of Defense, 2018d, p. 4. The recently initiated NMI on robotic process automation, which aims to automate back-end tasks to free up people to do more complicated tasks, is one current JAIC initiative in this direction.

within the FYDP. Finally, it would also likely improve visibility and communication by focusing the messaging.

In its role as the focal point of DoD's AI strategy tasked with scaling AI and its impact across DoD, and in tandem with its development of a five-year strategic plan as the first step of executing that mission (Recommendation T-1), the JAIC should either develop DoD-wide metrics by which to measure progress and communicate value or adopt and highlight some existing metrics if they fit the objective.[7] The JAIC council will be invaluable in that process. Because the DoD AI strategy's vision extends beyond developing technologies to transform DoD, so too should these metrics extend beyond the technology to assess its adoption and impact and the state of the ecosystem (e.g., infrastructure, AI talent, training) supporting this vision. The more easily these metrics can be tied to the overarching objective, the easier it will be to assess true progress toward the goal and to demonstrate value. Moreover, our industry interviews suggest the need for a baseline to compare with (see section "Industry: Organization" in Appendix C). It is therefore important for the JAIC to start thinking about the qualitative dimensions it aims to assess, potential metrics for those dimensions, and ways to quantitatively describe the current baseline, in tandem with the development of its five-year strategic road map.

Recommendation T-2: Each of the centralized AI service organizations should develop a five-year strategic road map, backed by baselines and metrics, to execute its mandate.

The evidence and motivation for Recommendation T-2, and the specific points therein, are parallel to those of our Recommendation T-1. We will not repeat them here. We will note, however, that the roles and mandates of the centralized AI service organizations will need to be defined or clarified to provide clarity and to enable the organizations to develop and execute meaningful road maps.

Recommendation T-3: The JAIC, working in partnership with the USD(R&E), the USD(A&S), the Chairman of the Joint Chiefs of Staff, and the service AI representatives on the JAIC

---

[7] It was not clear from our DoD interviews whether relevant metrics already exist, but we cannot rule them out either.

council, should carry out an annual or biannual portfolio review of DoD-wide investments in AI.

In its role of maintaining an accounting of DoD AI activity and enacting positive change given the requisite authorities (Recommendation S-1, Option 1 or Option 2), the JAIC needs to retain visibility into DoD's investments in AI; assess its alignment with DoD's vision; and enact change to enhance alignment and, ultimately, success. The summary of the 2018 DoD AI strategy stresses the "urgency, scale, and unity of effort needed to navigate this transformation."[8] Because of this, the overarching principle guiding DoD investments in AI should be to invest, as needed, to ensure the advancement and adoption of AI technologies at scale at the earliest possible time horizon across enterprise, mission-support, and operational AI for maximum positive mission impact. We recommend that the JAIC, working with relevant internal partners, carry out an annual or biannual portfolio review that would serve to assess alignment with this guiding principle, and for this review to identify gaps, barriers, and opportunities for redirection of activities to enhance alignment. The analysis we carried out for our portfolio review, described in the annex to this report, provides a potential starting point for such a portfolio review.

Recommendation T-4: The JAIC should organize a technical workshop, annually or biannually, showcasing AI programs DoD-wide.

Our industry interviews highlighted the need for a culture of openness and sharing to spur innovation and rapid advances, and a culture that tolerates failures, provided lessons are learned from it (see section "Industry: Innovation" in Appendix D). As the focal point of the DoD AI strategy, and in support of its role "synchronizing efforts and fostering collaboration," the JAIC has a role to play in bringing people together while developing a culture of openness and tolerance for experimentation and failure while learning.

We recommend that the JAIC organize a workshop bringing together the technical leads of AI activities across DoD. This workshop ideally would parallel and complement the annual or biannual

---

[8]   U.S. Department of Defense, 2018c, p. 4.

portfolio review activities (Recommendation T-3) and would serve as a platform to allow exchange of information and lessons learned, enhance cross-agency synergies, and provide visibility into the DoD portfolio of investments in AI to all stakeholders. It would also provide a mechanism for institutionalizing know-how and lessons learned. Beyond that, it would promote a culture of open sharing—if not outside DoD, at least within it.

Advancement and Adoption

Our next strategic recommendation, and the accompanying tactical one, addresses the question of VVT&E, which is highlighted in Chapters Three and Four and Appendixes B and C.

Recommendation S-2: DoD should advance the science and practice of VVT&E of AI systems, working in close partnership with industry and academia. The JAIC, working closely with USD(R&E), USD(A&S), and operational test and evaluation, should take the lead in coordinating this effort both internally and with external partners.

VVT&E is a critical consideration for DoD (see Chapter Three and Chapter Four), a significant challenge for the entire AI community (see Appendixes B and C), and a challenge that needs to be addressed, particularly as DoD looks to employ safety-critical AI systems.

VVT&E has multiple facets that need to advance: from foundational research to establish the theory and science of V&V and the theoretical underpinnings of T&E, to the development of standards, guidelines, and engineering best practices for the VVT&E of systems being fielded and operated. Because of this, multiple entities within DoD and the government have stakes in VVT&E and roles to play. Indeed, DARPA and the service labs have significant roles to play in establishing the science and its foundations, while the JAIC has a role to play in setting guidelines and institutionalizing best practices in DoD. NIST also has a role to play in developing nationwide standards. Likewise, multiple entities outside government have a stake and a role, including academics researching the science and developing the foundations and industry seeking to continue to leverage AI at scale.[9] In an ideal world, the theory and the science of VVT&E would come first. In practice, AI systems are currently being deployed, and it is therefore important to develop and institute practical alternatives, including best practices and guidelines, while waiting for the theory and science to mature.[10]

Leadership and open cooperation among the many stakeholders, at various levels, are required to overcome the challenge of advancing the science and practice of VVT&E. It behooves DoD to focus significant efforts and resources in this direction; to take a leadership role nationally in view of its reliance on safety-critical systems; to seek engagements and partnerships with all stakeholders in industry and academia to advance the science and practice of VVT&E; and to keep Congress informed of the status of DoD's activities, engagements, and partnerships in this regard. The JAIC should take the lead in spearheading coordination and keeping Congress informed of this national effort, both internally and with external partners.

Recommendation T-5: All funded AI efforts should include a budget for AI VVT&E.

This recommendation, in support of Recommendation S-2, is a forcing function that is relatively simple to implement and that can help ensure that the consideration of VVT&E is baked into the R&D of AI techniques and the design of AI solutions rather than considered as an afterthought further down the line. Although VVT&E during early R&D phases should be commonplace, we make this recommendation to explicitly reinforce its critical importance, to highlight the present lack of foundations for VVT&E in AI, and the importance of developing that science.

---

[9] Indeed, as we note in Chapter Three and Appendix C, the Partnership on AI—a technology-industry consortium focused on establishing best practices for AI—appears to be moving toward establishing engineering guidelines for certification of ML.

[10] Some of our industry interviewees indicated taking steps, internally and in industry partnerships, toward developing best practices (see Appendix C).

Our next recommendation is a tactical one, unrelated to VVT&E, but speaks to the need to bring developers of AI technologies together with users and operators to enable success in technology development.

Recommendation T-6: All agencies within DoD should create or strengthen mechanisms for connecting AI researchers, technology developers, and operators.

Historical precedents suggest that involving the operators and users in the development of technologies and the periodic development and reevaluation of CONOPs concurrently with technology development are fruitful endeavors (see section "The Offset Strategy" in Appendix D). In the case of AI, users and operators are critical because of the ideally spiral nature of AI development (see Chapter Three, section "Industry: Advancement and Adoption" in Appendix C, and section "Academia: Advancement and Adoption" in Appendix C). It is imperative to ensure the existence of mechanisms that enable tight feedback loops between the operators and the technologists at all stages, from early R&D to prototyping, experimentation, and development. These mechanisms are currently lacking (see section "Advancement and Adoption" in Chapter Four).

The mechanisms will likely be different for enterprise AI versus mission-support and operational AI. A possible option for enterprise AI would be the creation of focus groups of users, possibly domain-centric (e.g., financial management, health care management) across DoD and the services, to work with the technologists tasked with technology transfer or development. A possible option for both mission-support and operational AI would be the creation of an experimental unit within each service to experiment with technology prototypes. These would not be AI-specific units, but part of their charge would be experimenting with AI solutions in various scenarios. Such units would focus on testing and providing feedback on new technologies, starting from white-board concepts all the way to early- and late-stage prototypes. By getting operators involved early on in technological development, those operators can provide feedback to shape that development and develop the CONOPs and TTPs that make best use of these new technologies.

Innovation and Data

Our third strategic recommendation, and the accompanying tactical recommendation, address data as a critical resource for DoD, the need for a transformation in the overall culture of DoD to best leverage data, and potential avenues for enhancing innovation.

Recommendation S-3: DoD should recognize data as critical resources, continue instituting practices for their collection and curation, and increase sharing while resolving issues in protecting data after sharing and during analysis and use.

Data are critical resources and are not currently leveraged to their full potential in DoD (see Chapter Four). Remedying that requires DoD to institute processes, practices, and standards that encourage, if not require, the collection of data at every possible opportunity and that guide their preparation and curation. Remedying that also requires safeguarding the data as needed to protect sensitive data and to preserve access to data used in conjunction with the private sector. More fundamentally, DoD requires a significant cultural shift to develop a culture that recognizes the criticality of data and encourages sharing both internally and externally when advantageous to DoD.

The recent establishment of the CDO role within DoD is a big step in the right direction, enabling the establishment and diffusion of processes, practices, and standards. Likewise, the service CDOs have roles to play within their individual services. However, that is not enough, as a cultural shift is required in all parts, and at all levels, in DoD. Initiating that shift will likely require developing visible use cases (e.g., JAIC's NMIs) to demonstrate the value of data collection and curation for every opportunity across DoD.

Recommendation T-7: The CDO should consider making a selection of DoD data sets available to the AI community to spur innovation and enhance external engagement with DoD.

DoD faces stiff competition in a strong job market for AI talent (see Chapter Four) and should be looking for mechanisms to draw in talent and enhance external engagements and partnerships. Moreover, our academic and industry interviewees indicated that making data sets public provides a means to engage with partners and collaborators while spurring innovation in AI (see section "Industry: Data" in Appendix C, and section "Academia: Data" in Appendix C). In support of Recommendation S-4 and as a means of enhancing external innovation and external engagement with DoD, the CDO should consider making a selection of DoD data sets publicly available to the broader AI research community. These need not be data sets relating to critical DoD missions.

Talent

Our next strategic recommendation addresses the critical question of talent and points to a cultural shift that is needed to better enable DoD to access the AI talent pool.

Recommendation S-4: DoD should embrace permeability and an appropriate level of openness to enhance DoD's access to AI talent.

Regardless of the specific strategic road map taken, DoD's ability to scale AI will depend on its ability to consistently attract the right mix of AI talent in an extremely competitive AI market (see section "Talent" in Chapter Four, section "Talent" in Appendix B, section "Industry: Talent" in Appendix C, and section "Academia: Talent" in Appendix C). Our industry interviews highlight that AI talent (experts, developers, and program or project managers) expect to be changing roles or employers every two to four years (see section "Industry: Talent" in Appendix C). This competitive job market and the expectations of participants in it have forced various organizations to contend with a new reality. For example, our academic interviews highlighted that institutional flexibility, including allowing part-time (tenured) positions and extended sabbaticals, has been key to retaining AI faculty and research staff (see section "Academia: Talent" in Appendix C). In contrast, typical DoD career paths are longer and follow well-defined growth and advancement trajectories. DoD should neither expect nor necessarily want talent to remain in place for their entire careers, as this is inconsistent with the realities of the AI talent market and the current fast rate of technical advances in the field.

In theory, some permeability exists, most notably within the concept of *continuum of service,* to promote and support the management of the Reserve Components as an operational force.[11] In theory, the ability to hire Highly Qualified Experts also promotes permeability, bringing qualified civilians into the DoD workforce subject to a bound on the total number of civilians allowed DoD-wide.[12] In practice, based on our interviews within DoD (see section "Talent" in Appendix B) and recent testimony,[13] it is unclear whether these measures are sufficient to achieve the desired impact at scale. This situation, amplified by the realities of the tight AI job market, requires significant, serious measures. To address this reality, DoD should embrace permeability in many guises to enable AI talent to readily move in and out of civilian roles in DoD and enable more-fluid career paths within DoD (across civilian, reserve, and active duty posts).

Moreover, although, in principle, DoD should be able to attract AI talent on the basis of the attractiveness of the defense mission (see section "Thoughts Across Industry: On DoD Competing for AI Talent" in Appendix C), in practice, it is hard for AI talent to be drawn by the mission if they cannot talk about it or their roles in supporting it. Some levels of openness and transparency are likely needed—together with practices and processes that enable permeability—to ensure that DoD succeeds in competing in the AI talent market.

Connecting the Study Recommendations to the Congressional Language

The congressional language in Section 238(e) includes four recommendation elements, as follows:

---

[11] Department of Defense Directive 1200.17, *Managing the Reserve Components as an Operational Force,* Washington, D.C., October 29, 2008.

[12] Department of Defense Instruction 1400.25, *DoD Civilian Personnel Management System: Employment of Highly Qualified Experts (HQEs),* Washington, D.C., incorporating Change 1, January 18, 2017.

[13] David S. C. Chu, testimony before the National Commission on Military, National, and Public Service, Military Service Hearing, Washington, D.C., May 16, 2019.

Element (3)(B): Near-term actionable recommendations to the Secretary for the Department to secure and maintain technical advantage in artificial intelligence, including ways—

(i) to more effectively organize the Department for artificial intelligence;

(ii) to educate, recruit, and retain leading talent; and

(iii) to most effectively leverage investments in basic and advanced research and commercial progress in these technologies.

Element (3)(C): Recommendations on the establishment of Departmentwide data standards and the provision of incentives for the sharing of open training data, including those relevant for research into systems that integrate artificial intelligence and machine learning with human teams.

Element (3)(D): Recommendations for engagement by the Department with relevant agencies that will be involved with artificial intelligence in the future.

Element (3)(E): Recommendations for legislative action relating to artificial intelligence, machine learning, and associated technologies, including recommendations to more effectively fund and organize the Department.[14]

Table 5.1 indicates how the recommendations we lay out address (for strategic recommendations) or support (for tactical recommendations) those elements.

---

[14] Pub. L. 115–232, 2019.

Table 5.1
Connecting Study Recommendations to the Elements of Section 238(e) in the FY 2019 NDAA

Recommendation	Element (3)(B)(i)	Element (3)(B)(ii)	Element (3)(B)(iii)	Element (3)(C)	Element (3)(D)	Element (3)(E)
S-1	x					x
S-2			x		x	
S-3				x		
S-4		x				
T-1	x		x			
T-2	x		x			
T-3	x		x			
T-4	x	x				
T-5			x			
T-6			x			
T-7		x			x	

Details of the Analytic Methodology

As previously described in Chapter Two, we developed an analytical framework consisting of six dimensions along which to assess DoD's posture for AI. To carry out our assessment—and ultimately develop recommendations aiming to improve DoD's posture—we initiated four data-collection and analysis efforts, running mostly in parallel. Three of these efforts were exploratory and qualitative in nature (interviewing SMEs and stakeholders in DoD and other government agencies, interviewing experts in academia and private industry, and developing case studies), while the fourth consisted of a quantitative review of DoD's investment portfolio in AI. We then carried out an integrative analysis, bringing the first three lines of effort together to synthesize a holistic picture of the state of technology and DoD's posture, including current obstacles and friction points; and to develop recommendations that are both actionable and impactful. We opted to keep the fourth line of effort separate from the rest of the analysis and present it in a separate annex that is not publicly available, though it benefited from the insights into the conceptual framework that we proposed for DoD AI in Chapter Three.

In this appendix, we present the details of this analytic approach. We begin by individually describing the three exploratory data collection and analysis efforts—the details of the fourth line of effort are described in a separate annex associated with this report that is not available to the public. We then describe the integrative analysis undertaken to create a holistic picture of the current landscape. We will note that for purposes of execution, the team was divided into four subteams, in line with the four lines of effort: the government interview team, the academia and industry interview team, the case studies team, and the portfolio review team.

Exploratory Data Collection and Analysis Efforts

Overall Interview Approach

In preparation for our interview-based data collection efforts,[1] we carried out internal brainstorming sessions among the interview teams to develop a set of overarching questions for each of our six dimensions of posture assessment,[2] representing the main lines of inquiry we needed to follow to ascertain the current DoD posture. These questions served to guide our data-collection efforts by acting as broad themes in our interview protocols and also later to guide our data analysis efforts, for which these questions formed the basis of the first-level entries of the code tree we used to analyze the interview notes. We shall return to the code tree and its use at the end of this appendix.

Once these big questions were in place, we developed a set of generic interview protocols for our DoD interviews that were broadly aligned with types of interviewees (e.g., acquisition official, lab researcher, potential user). A member of RAND's Survey Research Group (SRG) reviewed these generic protocols. The SRG, established in 1972, is dedicated to ensuring that RAND research survey design, implementation, and data collection meet the high-quality standards set for all RAND research analytics; the SRG specializes in devising unique methods, including those aimed at accessing difficult-to-reach populations. For the current study, the SRG was asked to ensure that the surveys excluded closed-ended questions that could be answered by yes, no, or other one-word responses, and that they employed expansive questions that allowed interviewees to take the question in several

---

[1] This study was reviewed and determined to be exempt from human subjects review by RAND's National Security Research Division and by RAND's Human Subjects Protection Committee.

[2] We developed four to eight overarching questions per dimension.

directions. From these protocols, we later derived the protocols for the individual interviews by tweaking the questions to the interviewee or their organization, by emphasizing or deemphasizing certain parts of the relevant generic protocol, or by mixing and matching sections from multiple generic protocols. We also prepared brief read-aheads for our interviewees, consisting of a paragraph summarizing the study and its goals, and a half-dozen or so bullet points of broad discussion topics we wanted to focus on.

Because of the breadth of the study, the goals of this effort were not to develop a rigid set of questions or a rigid interview protocol to follow with all our interviewees. Rather, the goals were to solicit input covering the spectrum of topics we wished to explore, as opposed to soliciting multiple inputs on a given narrow question or set of questions. We therefore aimed to cast a wide net and ask a lot of complementary questions that, when pieced together collectively, would allow us to get a good overview of DoD's AI posture and activities.

In parallel with this preparation effort, we developed our wish list of interviewees across DoD. We will detail our selections and the underlying reasoning in the next section.

We then launched a series of semistructured interviews, approximately one hour in length, that sometimes turned into discussions. The RAND interview teams were advised to approach each interview with a prepared protocol but to remain flexible and open during the conversation. Sometimes interviewees had specific points or opinions that they were keen on sharing and that drove the meeting. Other times, their answers to interview questions inspired further questions that were not in the protocol we had prepared, and the interview team was encouraged to follow these threads.

Each interview was primarily focused on one or two dimensions of posture assessment, depending on the background and role of the interviewee. For consistency, we strove to ensure that the interview team member focusing on that dimension of the study was present at the interview. We also made sure interview teams consisted of at least two members and included a dedicated note-taker to capture the conversation to the extent possible. We opted not to record and then transcribe interviews to promote frank discussions and candid sharing of opinions.

The processes we used to prepare for our interviews within the federal government and in industry and academia were similar. Again, we prepared generic interview protocols for broad categories of interviewees (e.g., federal advisory board member, academic, strategy consultant), had them reviewed by a member of RAND's SRG to ensure adherence to our goals, and used them to derive the individual interview protocols. Our non-DoD interviews were staggered, by design, relative to our DoD interviews of similar experts, as we believed we were better able to target these interviews once we had a better sense of DoD's posture and activities.

Our rules of engagement for these interviews were as follows: We pledged not to identify individuals interviewed, cite or quote interviewees, or attribute anything they said to them or to their organizations. However, we clearly stated our intent to list each interviewee's organization.

Government Interviews

The RAND study team conducted 59 interviews within DoD and nine additional interviews within the federal government but outside DoD for a total of 68 federal government interviews. Nearly all the interviews were carried out in person; for logistical reasons, one DoD interview and two non-DoD interviews were carried out by phone, at the request of the interviewees. The first interview was held on February 27, 2019, and the last on August 29, 2019.

Our selection of DoD interviewees (Table 2.2 in Chapter Two) aimed to engage leadership aligned with each of the six dimensions of posture assessment and having a stake in AI, both within OSD and throughout the services. We also engaged with technical personnel (researchers, research leaders, and program managers) at the basic research arms of DoD. In particular, we attempted to maintain, to the extent possible, a parallel structure across the services when engaging with them: We aimed to speak to individuals with similar levels of seniority and in similar roles. That sometimes proved to be a challenge; the Navy and Marines, in particular, are organized differently from the

Air Force and Army. Finally, we sought to engage with leadership at federal agencies with involvement in AI and members of the relevant federal advisory bodies.

Academic and Industry Interviews

The RAND study team conducted 25 industry interviews and nine academic interviews (Table 2.3 in Chapter Two), covering a total of 29 and 10 interviewees, respectively. All the academic interviews were carried out in person. For logistical reasons, eight of our industry interviews were carried out by phone, and the remaining 17 were carried out in person. The first interview was held on May 15, 2019, and the last on September 3, 2019. These interviews were staggered, by design, relative to DoD interviews, to allow us to get a sense of DoD's current posture, and, accordingly, the types of questions that might be most interesting or relevant to pursue. Overall, securing interviews within DoD proved to be a much simpler task than securing interviews outside DoD.

In academia, we aimed to secure interviews at the universities with the highest-ranking graduate programs in computer engineering, CS, or electrical engineering, and with externally visible presence in AI, as exemplified by large AI labs or centers. To the top six schools that satisfied these criteria, we added Cornell Tech for its unique graduate education model fusing technology with business and entrepreneurship. The team typically met with prominent faculty members and researchers, some of whom were also in high-level leadership positions at their respective institutions. At two of the universities, our requests for interviews were routed to high-level administrators with nontechnical backgrounds but with AI involvement at their respective institutions.

In industry, we aimed to secure interviews at a selection of top technology companies (software and hardware) that are advancing the state of AI and its deployment at scale; the defense industrial base, for its traditional relevance to DoD; and top strategy consulting firms, for their perspective on scaling AI across traditional companies and organizations in many different industries. We also opted to target two types of commercial entities that we saw as having specific points of commonalities or parallels with DoD. First, we targeted large investment banks, because of the broad AI applications they employ. These applications might be viewed as parallel to the spectrum of enterprise, mission-support, and operational AI in DoD. Second, we targeted hospitals: Their historic use of heterogenous information technology (IT) infrastructure outsourced to multiple prime contractors and the emergence of centers of excellence that bring together AI researchers and medical professionals (users of AI) are both points of similarity with DoD. Our preference at the technology companies, defense industrial bases, and investment banks was to speak to senior AI or technical leadership. We were able to secure interviews accordingly for a majority of these organizations, with the exception of one. At the hospitals, we were able to secure interviews with medical doctors involved in AI research and technology leaders.

Historical Case Studies

We followed an exploratory case study methodology to develop six case studies. For each case study, we aimed to understand the how and why of events and to develop insights about the case study topic that might be relevant to one or more of our six dimensions of posture assessment.[3] We developed each of the case studies by mapping out a timeline of events based on multiple sources (primarily from the literature, and, in one instance, based on personal correspondence), developing a narrative of the history of the case, and extracting relevant insights about the case study topic along the relevant dimensions.

We did not carry out a multiple case-study analysis to compare or contrast across cases as is advised in the literature. Doing so would have required development of a theory and careful selection of cases such that the research team could predict similar results across cases or predict contrasting results based on that theory.[4] We did not have enough

---

[3] Pamela Baxter and Susan Jack, "Qualitative Case Study Methodology: Study Design and Implementation for Novice Researchers," *Qualitative Report*, Vol. 13, No. 4, December 1, 2008, p. 548, Table 2.

[4] Robert K. Yin, *Case Study Research: Design and Methods*, 3rd ed., Thousand Oaks, Calif.: SAGE Publications, 2003.

information at the start of the project to suggest a theory, and the six case studies considered (chosen as described next) were sufficiently different that a comparison across the case studies was not particularly meaningful. Therefore, we treated the case studies as six separate cases, each leading to insights aligned with one or more dimensions of our posture assessment. Those insights were then used as additional evidence to supplement the evidence collected from other data sources for that particular dimension.

To choose cases for study (that is, choose the case units of analyses), we began by polling our RAND colleagues for suggestions. The colleagues we polled had a variety of experiences and backgrounds, including data scientists and engineers with expertise in AI, former government policymakers with experience in cyber, acquisition experts, researchers with backgrounds in intelligence policy, and researchers with background in environmental studies. Specifically, we asked them to suggest cases where DoD or a similar government agency had to posture to build, procure, transition, test, operate, or sustain a type of capability. Next, we applied our own judgment to assess which of the six focus areas would likely be informed by each suggested case. As a final step, we selected a subset of six cases that could be studied within the available time and resources of the project and that were collectively expected to span all six dimensions of the posture assessment.[5] We conducted the following case studies: AI history in DoD; the history of software development in DoD; DoD posture for cyber; the offset strategy; the adoption and scaling of unmanned aircraft systems (UAS); and Big Safari (see Appendix D).

The case studies team members were provided materials adapted from the relevant literature to familiarize themselves with different types of biases that might affect their work and with bias-mitigation techniques for avoiding them.[6] The researchers were instructed to seek

---

[5] We emphasize here that there is no direct connection between the number of dimensions of posture assessment and the number of case studies ultimately pursued—that the two numbers match is a coincidence.

[6] Lisa Krizan, "Intelligence Essentials for Everyone," Occasional Paper, No. 6, Washington, D.C.: Joint Military Intelligence College, June 1999.

sources with confirmatory and critical viewpoints to help avoid premature formation of views in deriving insights from their case studies, and to avoid deriving superficial lessons from history. They were also encouraged to consider inclusion of alternative views in developing their narrative. Finally, we also submitted early writeups of the case studies to an informal peer review as an additional step to help mitigate research bias.

Coding Approach

We used a software program (Dedoose) to systematically analyze the notes collected during our interviews. We began by developing a code tree, shown in Box A.1, for coding and organizing the notes. The top-level nodes of the code tree are aligned with our six dimensions of posture assessment. We added two additional sets of top-level nodes: One covered the conceptualization of AI because of the prevalence of that topic in our interviews, and the second covered congressional actions and legislation to capture the topic when it arose. We then used the big questions developed at the onset of the study and that formed the basis of the interview protocols to add a second level to the code tree to capture the primary topics of interest. We added a tertiary layer of codes to elicit current DoD status, industry status, and thoughts about what DoD should be doing.

To promote consistency, we used a codebook (based on the code tree shown in Box A.1) in Dedoose, and we formalized a multistep procedure for coding our interviews. In the first step, the main interviewer identified excerpts associated with the top-level codes. In the second step, the leads for each dimension coded the excerpts associated with their dimension across all interviews, adding codes at lower depths of the code tree as appropriate. This ensured that only one person used the lower-level codes associated with each dimension of posture assessment, so that we did not have to worry about intercoder reliability. The third step was freeform. The leads for each dimension were encouraged to add memos highlighting emerging themes that they noticed from their interviews, and other members of the team were encouraged to note supporting material as appropriate. This gave them an opportunity to highlight themes that they noticed outside the rigorous structure imposed by the code tree and corresponding code book.

Integrative Analysis

The study leaned heavily, but not solely, on qualitative data-collection efforts through interviews and discussions with varied audiences. The coding system described above allowed us to organize and analyze several hundred pages of interview notes, providing a broad perspective. Our goal was to capture, sift through, and analyze as broad a perspective as possible, in line with the congressional language.

From this process, we were able to derive a picture of DoD's current posture and activities in AI. By combining lessons learned from the industry and academic interviews, supplemented with insights garnered from the case studies, our team's technical and other expertise, and opportunistic consultation of the literature, we were able to derive recommendations for DoD. Although the process of documenting and organizing the meeting notes was systematic, there were ultimately informed judgments to be made at various steps. For example, we had to make informed judgments about what was important: We always deemed recurring themes important, but we sometimes highlighted or otherwise took into account less-prevalent ones as well. For recurring opinions, we had to make informed judgments about whether they were correct.[7] When opinions conflicted, we had to make informed conclusions where possible. Finally, we had to make informed conclusions on what lessons or insights could be extrapolated to DoD and its mission or for AI, as not everything that is true for academia or industry is true for DoD, and not everything that is true for other technologies, particularly hardware-heavy ones, is true for AI.

---

[7] As an example of an incorrect but nonetheless prevalent opinion, our interviewees often conflated AI V&V with software verification. The technical expertise resident in the team allowed us to resolve this.

Although DoD interviewees often but not always agreed on perceived obstacles and friction points, they often disagreed on potential solutions and their merits, sometimes even within the same organization. Even when interviewees agreed, it was not always clear that the consensus opinion would bring about the desired result. Additionally, the applicability of perspectives or insights from industry, academia, historical case studies, and even other federal experiences had to be carefully weighed and evaluated against DoD's mission and culture. The broad view of the landscape provided by our interviewees enabled the study team to draw informed conclusions, using the data collected through the interviews augmented by the team's own expertise and consultation of the relevant literature.,

---

Box A.1. Code Tree for 2019 RAND Section 238(e) Study Interviews

1. Conceptualization of AI
   1.1 What AI means to the interviewee
   1.2 Need for a DoD-wide definition of AI

2. Organization
   2.1 Why DoD should be posturing for AI
   2.2 Strategy and measures of success
      2.2.1 DoD strategy and measures of success
      2.2.2 Strategy and measures of success in non-DoD organizations
      2.2.3 What the DoD strategy should be; how DoD should define and measure success
   2.3 Organizational structure; stakeholders and their stakes, mandates, roles, and authorities
      2.3.1 What they are within DoD
      2.3.2 What they are within non-DoD organizations
      2.3.3 What they should be within DoD
   2.4 Stakeholder roles and their execution; how stakeholders and their roles interact
      2.4.1 Within DoD; enablers, obstacles
      2.4.2 Within non-DoD organizations; enablers, obstacles, best practices, and lessons learned

Box A.1—Continued

2.4.3 What they are between DoD and non-DoD organizations
2.4.4 What the roles and their execution should be within DoD
2.4.5 How DoD stakeholders should interact/partner with non-DoD organizations

3. Advancement
  3.1 State of AI, its future prospects, and relevance for DoD
    3.1.1 Currently ripe and mature AI technologies, DoD relevance
    3.1.2 Predictions on future technologies and their timelines, DoD relevance
    3.1.3 Current state of VVT&E for AI
      3.1.3.1 Needs and capabilities (present or anticipated/desired) within DoD
      3.1.3.2 How non-DoD organizations ensure AI technologies perform as desired
  3.2 R&D investments in AI; construction and balancing of the AI R&D portfolio
    3.2.1 DoD R&D investments and why; how the portfolio is constructed and balanced
    3.2.2 AI investments in non-DoD organizations; construction of the AI portfolio, what drives it
    3.2.3 What DoD AI R&D portfolio should be and why
    3.2.4 Where DoD-led investment in AI is needed and why
  3.3 Coordinating AI R&D efforts
    3.3.1 How DoD coordinates its AI R&D efforts, internally and externally
    3.3.2 How non-DoD organizations coordinate their AI R&D efforts internally and externally
    3.3.3 How DoD should be coordinating its AI R&D efforts
      3.3.3.1 Internally, among DoD stakeholders
      3.3.3.2 Externally, with other federal agencies, industry, and academia

4. Adoption
  4.1 Specific AI technologies DoD is currently looking to acquire and why
  4.2 Overcoming the valley of death in AI

Box A.1—Continued

4.2.1 Root causes of the valley of death within DoD, especially in AI

4.2.2 How non-DoD organizations connect research to end products/business

4.2.3 How DoD might overcome the valley of death in AI

4.3 Acquisition of AI technologies

    4.3.1 How DoD acquires AI; enablers and obstacles

    4.3.2 How non-DoD organizations acquire AI; enablers, obstacles, and solutions

        4.3.2.1 How non-DoD organizations decide on what to acquire versus build in-house

    4.3.3 How DoD should be acquiring AI; changes and solutions and why

4.4 Sustainment of AI technologies

    4.4.1 How DoD fields and sustains AI; enablers and obstacles

    4.4.2 How non-DoD organizations field and sustain AI; enablers, obstacles, and solutions

    4.4.3 How DoD should be fielding and sustaining AI and why

4.5 Enhancing adoption of AI

    4.5.1 How DoD is changing doctrine, CONOPs, TTPs, or business processes

    4.5.2 How non-DoD organizations update business processes for AI

    4.5.3 How DoD should change doctrine, CONOPs, TTPs, or business practices

5. Innovation

  5.1 What innovation means

    5.1.1 Within DoD

    5.1.2 Outside the DoD

  5.2 Internal innovation

    5.2.1 How DoD fosters it; enablers and obstacles

    5.2.2 How non-DoD organizations foster it; enablers, obstacles, and solutions

    5.2.3 How DoD should be fostering internal innovation

  5.3 Leveraging external innovation

    5.3.1 DoD mechanisms to bring in external innovation; enablers and obstacles

Box A.1—Continued

5.3.2.1 How DoD entities work together to leverage external innovation

5.3.2 How non-DoD organizations bring in and leverage external innovation

5.3.3 How DoD might further leverage external innovation

6. Data

  6.1 Data needs, availability, and governance

  6.1.1 Data needs within DoD and why

  6.1.2 Data availability and governance within the DoD; obstacles and enablers

  6.1.3 Data needs, availability, and governance within non-DoD organizations; best practices

  6.1.4 How DoD should be collecting and governing data

  6.2 Infrastructure for storage, compute, communication

  6.2.1 Status of DoD infrastructure; obstacles and enablers

  6.2.2 Status of non-DoD infrastructure; lessons learned and best practices

  6.2.3 What infrastructure DoD should have

  6.3 Information security

  6.3.1 Within DoD; needs, current approaches, and limitations

  6.3.2 Within non-DoD organizations; needs and current approaches

  6.3.3 How DoD should approach information security

7. Talent

  7.1 AI talent needs

  7.1.1 Types of AI talent needed within DoD and why

  7.1.2 Types of AI talent needed within non-DOD organizations and why

  7.2 Career paths for AI talent and means of tracking them

  7.2.1 Within DoD; obstacles and enablers

  7.2.2 Within non-DoD organizations; obstacles, solutions, and enablers

  7.2.3 What they should be within DoD; how to overcome current obstacles

  7.3 Hiring and retention

  7.3.1 How DoD accesses and retains AI talent; obstacles

Box A.1—Continued

7.3.2 How non-DoD organizations hire and retain AI talent; obstacles and enablers
7.3.3 How DoD can better compete in accessing and retaining AI talent
7.4 Training needs and approaches for AI talent and AI users
7.4.1 Training needs within DoD and why
7.4.2 Training needs within non-DoD organizations and why; current training offerings
7.4.3 How DoD can enhance training internally
7.4.4 How DoD and non-DoD organizations can partner to enhance DoD training

8. Congressional actions or legislation
8.1 Concerns or fears about regulatory actions
8.2 Desired regulatory actions

Insights from Federal Interviews

In this appendix, we summarize the insights gleaned from our federal interviews, within and outside DoD, along the six dimensions of our posture assessment. Some of these insights are factual statements about DoD or other activities; others reflect opinions expressed. Where factual statements are concerned, we report them as we understood them to be true at the time of the interviews. Where opinions are concerned, we have aimed to highlight themes that recur in multiple interviews; with few exceptions, we do not attempt to capture the theme's prevalence, instead using the word "some" to indicate a theme present across several interviews. Where we do report prevalence (using such words as "most" or "consensus"), we have attempted to clarify the relevant sample size. We also report opinions that, although not recurring, we deemed important for offering an interesting perspective or a creative approach that might be valuable. We use the word "one" to indicate such opinions.

Organization

At the OSD Level

The JAIC was established in July 2018 as the focal point of AI within DoD. We learned from our interviews that its initial staffing consisted primarily of officers detailed from the services for six months. At the time of our interviews, the JAIC was expecting a 70-percent turnover in personnel. The JAIC had secured 75 billets for FY 2020, of which 59 would be allocated to civilian personnel and 16 to military personnel.

The next round of detailees are expected to carry out 12-month tours. We also learned from our interviews that the talent pool appears to be uneven, with many applicants for policy roles and a scarce number of applicants for technical roles. The JAIC has since hired a new chief science officer, a new chief technology officer, and a new chief of acquisitions.

Our interviewees within the Office of the CIO appeared to have a clear vision for the JAIC; its role in accelerating the adoption of AI by getting it to work at scale; and its role in establishing common foundations, governance, authorities, policies, outreach, and external engagements and in forging relationships and institutionalizing lessons learned. Interviewees also appeared to expect the JAIC to change and evolve as it finds it way forward. What was less clear to us from these interviews was the extent of the JAIC's role in synchronizing AI programs across DoD (and the mechanisms, if any, for doing so).

In contrast, understanding of and expectations for the JAIC's mandate and roles among our interviewees in the federal government (outside the JAIC) varied widely. Some interviewees called for clarity around the JAIC's mandate, its role in DoD AI, and how it fits within the wider OSD ecosystem, particularly USD(R&E) and USD(A&S). Additionally, interviewees had very different ideas—sometimes even within the same organization—about what the JAIC should be, ranging from a field agency with significant authorities to a center of excellence with a specific focus and minimal authorities (e.g., VVT&E standards, 6.4-appropriated programs and beyond, policies and governance). One of our interviewees suggested elevating AI to a major force program.

We noted enthusiasm among our DoD interviews for the JCF, with an extensive wish list for the JAIC. These included calls for the JAIC to help overcome barriers in securing an authority to operate; calls for deploying "carrots and sticks" to motivate data sharing across DoD; calls for development of a library of common algorithms for DoD; calls for reinforcing data access restrictions in a common way across DoD; calls for developing standardized data query and visualization tools across DoD; and calls for developing uniform policies for sandboxing. In contrast, support for the JAIC's NMIs and their selection varied widely among interviewees across DoD, with less enthusiasm noted overall than for the JCF.

Within the Services

We learned from our interviews that the Air Force has an AI CFT that was co-led by an Air Force captain (company grade officer rank, O-3 pay grade).[1] Its mandate and role are not specified in the publicly available Air Force AI strategy annex, and we do not have access to the Appendix referenced therein.[2] Based on our interviews, the Air Force AI CFT played a role in establishing the MIT–Air Force AI Accelerator, had a role interfacing with the AFRL, and was tasked with interfacing with the JAIC. At the time of our interviews, the colead was moving on shortly, and it was unclear from our interviews what would happen to the AI CFT at that point. The authorities of the Air Force AI CFT were unclear from our interviews.

The Army's AI Task Force is part of the recently established AFC and is headed by a brigadier general (one-star general officer, O-7 pay grade) who reports directly to the AFC deputy commanding general for combat development, with additional dotted lines of reporting to the assistant secretary of the Army for acquisition, logistics, and technology and the AFC deputy commanding general for futures and concepts. The AI Task Force follows a hub-and-spokes model, with the hub headquartered at CMU. Based on our interviews, the AI Task Force appears to be a cross between an organizational entity modeled after the JAIC and a CFT that works in tandem with AFC's other CFTs. The authorities of the AI Task Force, and its ability to direct AI projects across the Army, appeared limited, according to our interviews. Its placement within AFC might also pose barriers for collaboration or coordination with the Office of Business Transformation, where some of the enterprise AI applications in the Army are likely to reside.

The Navy's AI Task Force is led by a rear admiral (two-star flag officer, O-8 pay grade) who concurrently serves as the chief of naval research and director, Innovation Technology Requirements, and

---

[1] This information was accurate as of the last interview, which was held August 23, 2019.

[2] U.S. Department of the Air Force, 2019.

Test and Evaluation (OPNAV-N94). The Navy AI Task Force draws together subject-matter experts from the Navy commands and elements of the Marine Corps and Secretariat. It is working to address warfighting, training, and corporate problems in AI, though based on our interviews, its precise role and mandate remain unclear. We are also unable to ascertain the authorities of the Navy AI Task Force within this organizational construct. Although the study team viewed a predecisional draft of a Navy AI annex that is not available to the general public, we have not been able to ascertain whether the annex was finalized and released. Nonetheless, our understanding was that the Navy AI strategy is (at least partially) driven by an unclassified document.[3] Finally, one of our Navy interviewees mentioned an "AI readiness score card," though in our interview we were unable to ascertain the details, or its relevance to establishing potential metrics for success.

The Marines have also stood up an AI Task Force, headed by a civilian member of the Senior Executive Service who reports to the deputy commandant for information. Based on our interviews, the Marines AI Task Force focuses on identifying and seeking prototypes and solutions for specific use cases and developing best practices and policies for AI governance. The authorities of the Marines AI Task Force were unclear from our interviews. However, we will note that in contrast to the other services, it appears that the Marines AI Task Force was not tasked with interfacing with the JAIC.

Finally, the Department of the Navy (DON) did not have a stand-alone AI strategy.[4] Moreover, it was in the midst of an extensive digital reorganization that saw the creation of a newly appointed DON CIO, a chief technology officer, a CDO, a chief digital innovation officer, and a chief information security officer. It is unclear how that will ultimately influence the DON's organizational or governance structures for AI, if any.

---

[3] Chief of Naval Operations, U.S. Navy, *A Design for Maintaining Maritime Superiority*, version 2.0, Washington, D.C., December 2018, p. 11.

[4] This information is accurate as of our last inquiry on October 17, 2019.

Advancement and Adoption

Some of our technical interviewees in DoD were concerned that military leaders without technical backgrounds greatly overestimate current AI capabilities and think of AI as a magic bullet. Two interviewees mentioned feeling pressure from senior military leadership to focus solely on operational AI capabilities. One interviewee noted that the deployment of operational AI might suffer from less red tape than that of enterprise AI, because changes to warfighting are easier to push through DoD bureaucracy than are changes to business processes. A recurring theme among these interviewees was that AI is a tool that, like any other tool, has strengths and weaknesses and is useful to employ in some situations but not in others.

The consensus among our interview subjects with technical backgrounds was that enterprise AI is closer to deployment than is mission-support AI, with operational AI the furthest out. That view was reported in 15 of our interviews, and a much smaller number (three interviews) noted that there is low-hanging fruit in all three categories, with ISR, PM, and intelligence analysis considered to be some of the most promising applications outside enterprise AI. No interviewees thought that operational AI will be deployed at scale sooner than will enterprise AI, but interviewees agreed that, in the long run, all three categories of AI are likely to deliver enormous advantages to DoD.

Although enterprise AI was viewed to be the technological low-hanging fruit for DoD, none of the service lab researchers interviewed were working on it, with some noting that many enterprise applications are already available from the private sector. Rather, these researchers were working on a variety of applications across mission-support and operational AI, and performing basic research on alternative AI paradigms to traditional DL. One interviewee suggested that DoD will need to lead in researching AI at the "tactical edge," out of contact with large data centers with abundant computing hardware.

Interviewees felt that most of the near-term applications will use supervised DL, but cautioned that this could easily change in the future and that DoD should not get locked into any one particular AI technology. Some interviewees noted that before AI can become useable in real-time operations, there needs to be further research into human-machine interaction (e.g., taking into account the operator's emotional state). One interviewee predicted that as training algorithms improve, ML will require less training data, so the relative balance of importance will shift away from data quantity and more toward skilled talent and computational resources. Some interviewees felt that there have been few fundamental advances in AI algorithms in the past 30 years, with most of the recent developments coming from increased data and computational power.

There was consensus among our technical interviewees that the AI community does not have reliable methods for VVT&E of AI systems, and that the methods that do exist are nowhere near enough to guarantee the performance of AI in safety-critical situations, as noted in 16 interviews. This was given as one major reason why operational AI is not yet near readiness for deployment. One interviewee mused that the large "AI native" companies are probably the world leaders on this front, and probably have proprietary VVT&E practices that are better than the publicly available ones.[5] Only one interviewee expressed the belief that DoD should take more risks with deploying AI whose safety cannot be guaranteed, in strong contrast to the views held by our other technical interviewees. Two interviewees noted that VVT&E needs to be repeated every time an ML algorithm is retrained, which adds additional complexity.

All eight interviewees who were asked about adversarial attacks against AI considered it to be a serious problem with no clear technological solutions. Some of these interviewees predicted that adversarial AI will remain a "cat-and-mouse game" of incremental advances in both offense and defense as long as ML remains the dominant AI paradigm. One interviewee expressed the belief that the biggest concern was not adversarial attacks that trick the AI system in highly controlled ways, but rather attacks that generally confuse it and cause it to behave in ways that are unpredictable to either the operator or the attacker.

Some technical interviewees expressed strong beliefs that the slow and somewhat linear RDT&E model specified by the 6.1–6.7 appro-

---

[5]   We note that this view was not supported by our industry interviews, where interviewees likewise flagged VVT&E as a serious open problem (see section "Industry: Advancement and Adoption" in Appendix C).

priations system (which was designed for large hardware projects) is not the right model for AI development, primarily because of the speed at which AI technology is advancing. They advocated a more flexible model with strong collaboration between the developer and the end user during the development stage, and with an emphasis on rapid attainment of a minimum viable product and continuous user feedback. Two interviewees specifically endorsed the recommendations of the DIB's 2019 SWAP Study.[6]

Interviewees noted that there are few formal channels for coordination and deconfliction of AI R&D between DoD components, although there is significant informal coordination through personal contacts. Some thought that this informal system works fairly well while others felt that information remains excessively siloed. Interviewees were generally open to the possibility of establishing more-formal coordination and deconfliction channels, but cautioned that this would be useful only if the components see a personal benefit from participating, and that such an effort would fail if it were simply mandated from above or if R&D decisionmaking became centralized.

Our interviewees from the acquisition and operator communities generally agreed that AI is not a stand-alone capability but one that is pervasive in many systems, and that DoD personnel need to become comfortable with the technology, a task that will require some effort. One interviewee noted widespread fear that advances in AI will eliminate human jobs rather than freeing human beings to focus on more-substantive work or perform their current functions more effectively, and another interviewee noted concerns that people might not be able to interact with AI technologies synergistically in combat environments. Such anxieties appeared to be less pronounced among younger officers who, as digital natives, expect that they will be using the latest technologies during their service. One interviewee noted that Marines might be less predisposed to see advances in AI as intrinsically threatening, because they are accustomed to being placed in and adapting to unfamiliar environments. Some interviewees expressed the belief that DoD should introduce AI incrementally to alleviate resistance to it.

---

[6] DIB, 2019b.

One interviewee even encouraged service chiefs to enlist science-fiction writers in communicating the importance of AI adoption to service members and allaying concerns they might have.

A recurring concern among these interviewees were DoD's acquisitions processes, which date back to the Cold War and were designed with hardware, not software, in mind.[7] One interviewee noted that even rapid acquisition can actually take up to two years, and another estimated that those processes have left the United States some two decades behind other major AI players in securing and incorporating the latest advances. Several interviewees stated that DoD could adopt AI technologies more quickly and enhance its ability to secure industry partners were it to procure those technologies in accordance with existing commercial standards. One interviewee noted that DoD too often ends up creating onerous adoption requirements that, when enacted, already lag their industry counterparts by five years, and another noted that DoD should consider treating AI technologies like perishable goods that might well have wilted by the time they have been acquired. A third described the ideal acquisition process as "Start small, iterate frequently, and terminate frequently." Another interviewee noted that DoD has some agile components—Kessel Run, notably—but as a whole, DoD remains ill suited to incorporating the latest advances in AI, which largely come from smaller companies, not established titans in the defense industrial base.

Innovation

Although AI innovation was important to DoD research organizations we spoke to, each organization approached fostering internal innovation in a different way, largely dependent on available resources and the leadership and size of each organization. Despite differences, interviewees emphasized that it was important to innovation to have the

---

[7] We note here the similarity in concerns expressed about the DoD acquisition process among our technical interviewees, summarized earlier, and our interviewees in the acquisition and operator communities.

flexibility to pursue research questions freely. Interviewees also stated the importance of building a team with a variety of experiences and expertise to address a wide variety of research issues.

Throughout our interviews, participants highlighted several issues and inhibitors. For example, it was noted that DoD lacks long-term strategy to drive innovation and impact. Some interviewees also stated that much of the research they do is not risky or innovative. Interviewees noted that flows of information between researchers and other parts of their organizations can be very siloed, and this can hinder innovation itself and awareness of opportunities to bring in innovation. Interviewees cited concerns about funding, referencing issues with confusion over which appropriation their research fell under (e.g., 6.1, 6.2) even after a funding source had been identified. Some interviewees also expressed the belief that overclassification of data and information presented innovation barriers. Finally, a lack of bandwidth owing to their many tasks was also cited as an inhibitor to innovation.

Several DoD organizations we interviewed interact with personnel at domestic universities, research institutions, and in industry, and at international universities and organizations as a means of exchanging ideas and bringing in innovation. Some interviewees stated that they attend various technology conferences to connect with others in the AI field, such as researchers at universities or international organizations. Personal connections were very important to bringing in innovation, and many interviewees relied on personal relationships with others at academic institutions and in industry to bring in innovation. Some, when asked, admitted that a network based on personal connections was likely not sustainable in the long term, but interviewees were not sure that formalized connections would help. Some expressed resistance to the idea of a formalized means of interaction. The main reason for resistance is a belief that this would only result in more meetings and bureaucratic oversight but would not actually improve cross-organizational communication.

Despite this concern, some interviewees felt that more should be done to bring in external innovation. For example, one suggestion was to fully use alliances with U.S. foreign partners, such as Japan, Israel, and India, to bring in additional innovation. Overall, interviewees expressed the belief that the ability to bring in innovation from the private sector and other external sources is extremely important. They cited that not everything can or should be done in-house; that it is important to be able to leverage capabilities developed by non-DoD government organizations and outside the government. Some interviewees also spoke about negative civilian perceptions of DoD and the effect that these perceptions have on DoD's ability to bring in innovation, citing an unwillingness among some in academia and the private sector to work with DoD.

Data

Several interviewees expressed the opinion that DoD is facing a data crisis that takes many forms. According to them, leaders throughout the Pentagon find themselves unable to rely on the facts and figures they are presented with, because too often a figure presented as a fact in one presentation will quickly be contradicted by a different figure for the same fact in a subsequent presentation. When leaders or analysts want to answer a question about DoD or its operations through data, they frequently find that it will take most of a year to gain access to the data they need to answer it, and even once they obtain access, understanding what the data mean and how they are structured can take as long as six months. Even worse, data collected by different systems are rarely interoperable, which means that data captured by one system have not been designed to align with data collected by other systems. Because DoD operates many tens of thousands of software applications, most questions from leadership require the analysis of data captured by more than one system to answer them, and combining data from more than one system frequently presents a major challenge.

DoD also lacks a systematic approach for its personnel to discover what data it gathers and whether those data might be relevant to any particular problem or concern. It also lacks easy access to the cheap and plentiful data storage capabilities that have become commonplace in the private sector through the widespread adoption of cloud-based data storage. Indeed, most software applications in DoD treat storage capacity as a scarce resource, and store data only when DoD sees an immediate need for the efficient functioning of narrow use cases.

A primary lesson from early DoD experiments with AI, including Project Maven and PM projects, is that the present state of data within DoD represents a significant barrier to more-rapid progress and more-useful algorithms.

DoD's primary response to these challenges appears to have been to consolidate its operations. First, DoD is attempting to reduce the number of discrete data centers and consolidate the locations of the computers that physically power its software infrastructure into fewer but larger data centers. Second, DoD is attempting to reduce the tens of thousands of software applications that support its various enterprise business processes by reducing the number of officially supported and maintained applications, often working to reduce the number of software applications operating in a functional area from hundreds to merely dozens.

Interviewees proposed a few different solutions to their problems with data. One proposed solution is for DoD to acquire the cheap, always available storage solutions already available in the private sector. A second proposed solution is for all software applications used by any part of DoD to emphasize interoperability regarding its data. A third proposed solution is for data professionals within DoD to form a stronger community, as DoD personnel often find themselves facing similar problems but have no way to find shared solutions or learn from the successful efforts of others. Some interviewees expressed a desire for an environment for their own work that resembles GitHub or Stack Overflow—where private-sector software developers share tools, tips, and best practices.

Finally, interviewees noted that some parts of DoD have had success identifying key business scenarios to focus their modernization efforts. For example, some noted that Congress's focus on the auditability of DoD's financial management practices has resulted in somewhat better data quality and interoperability in this functional area of each of the services compared with other business functions. Interviewees suggested that establishing appropriate focal goals for each of the major DoD enterprise functions and measuring progress against them over an extended timeframe could provide a similar guidepost to direct long-term improvements in DoD's data infrastructure, improvements that would endure beyond the tenure of any particular set of DoD leaders. Interviewees also noted that providing seed funding for projects aimed at advancing these goals, even if such funding is inadequate to fund the entire cost of improvement projects, would likely speed efforts as well.

The question of data ownership was also brought up by some interviewees as an unsolved problem.

Talent

A couple of our interviewees hinted at the dearth of technical talent within OSD. One noted that the Army currently has less than 500 data scientists, and another noted that less than 5 percent of the Air Force's personnel have STEM backgrounds.

Interviewees across DoD did not have a clear or consistent definition of AI talent, with the exception of interviewees more actively engaged with AI, such as in the research labs. However, these interviewees were also more likely to interpret "AI talent" as talent needed for the development of AI. These interviewees believed an advanced technical degree was required, along with strong computer programming skills and noncognitive skills such as critical thinking and problem-solving. They did not believe that having a degree alone was sufficient.

In contrast, interviewees who did not actively work in or with AI were more likely to discuss technical talent—particularly cyber talent—as an analog or proxy for AI talent. Cyber talent was an easier occupational field for discussion in these cases, because DoD has spent the past five years reclassifying and managing its uniformed and civilian cyber workforce. Many interviewees also discussed data scientists as AI talent. Those interviewees, who were more removed from AI, such as in personnel management, were less likely to believe that there was an urgent need for AI to be recognized as a separate occupational group.

Interviewees also had different ideas about AI talent needs. Some interviewees discussed AI talent within DoD more broadly while others focused on their service, command, or group. Interviewees providing broad comments were more likely to discuss a general need for people with AI skills, and a lack of current capabilities within DoD, without getting into specifics. Those speaking at the services or group level, particularly those engaged with AI development, were more likely to have the view that there was a need for technical talent, particularly those able to code and do advanced data analytics. They also expressed a need for individuals who can make existing data ready for AI (i.e., data engineers). Much of this variation speaks to how talent is currently managed at DoD, the role of personnel offices at the OSD and services levels, and the role and availability of direct hiring authorities.

Moreover, there were differences of opinion among our interviewees around the type of AI talent needed by DoD. At the core of this conversation is an open question about whether DoD should be developing or acquiring AI. There was further nuance in our conversation regarding the types of AI applications considered. For example, some interviewees believed that the development of operational AI should be done in-house with their service organization in charge of development. Other interviewees expressed the belief that contractors were better positioned to develop AI, and that it was not an area of competitive advantage for DoD, nor should it be. These interviewees emphasized the need for AI expertise in acquisition and program management, although they acknowledged few people had this combination of skills.

Because there are currently no AI-specific occupations in the uniformed or civilian service, there is currently no formal tracking of AI talent in DoD. As a result, the few who are working in AI are currently classified across occupational codes. AI technical talent is currently found across different specialties (e.g., operations researchers, program analysts and managers, scientists, cyber specialists, engineers). Some interviewees expressed the opinion that AI development and application is a team effort, and that several occupational types along the development and validation process are required to build and apply AI.

We learned from our interviews that organizations engaged in AI development, such as the service labs, are informally tracking AI talent. These include efforts to identify talent with AI-relevant skills and those that could be cross-trained to work on AI projects. We also heard that the services more generally are undertaking servicewide initiatives to better identify those with technical skills—for example, through the creation of proficiency tests in the Air Force and through creating a skills repository for officers in the Army.

Importantly, some interviewees noted that technical career tracks are not well delineated in terms of opportunities and progression of assignments. There was a perception that although these are critical fields, more-technical tracks had limited promotion potential. Interviewees believed this was ingrained in military culture and would be challenging to adjust.

A widely shared view was that it is difficult to find, attract, and cultivate technical talent, including AI talent. For interviewees actively engaged in AI development, there was an emphasis on the use of informal networks in industry and academia. Research labs, which have direct hiring authorities, also cited hosting competitions and other events, along with sponsoring postdoctoral fellowships, as ways to attract AI talent. Interviewees also noted that mission and the ability to work on interesting and impactful problems would drive DoD's competitiveness as an employer.

Some interviewees emphasized the importance of "permeability"— the ability of individuals with valuable skills to easily transition among the active, reserve, and civilian components. There was recognition that few people remain in the same job for their entire career and that this could be used to DoD's advantage. Interviewees who supported greater permeability also saw the value of having talent rotate back and forth from the private sector as a means of enabling talent to refresh their skills in an environment on the cutting edge of AI and to bring back the latest expertise to DoD.

Notably, interviewees in personnel policy were less likely to believe that there was an urgent need for any military or civilian policy changes to better attract AI talent. These interviewees believed existing flexibilities for hiring and incentives for pay were sufficient, and that services could leverage them for AI talent. Among the most-cited flexibilities were those specific to technical talent: the new Cyber Excepted Service for civilian hires, and the recent changes to the Defense Officer Personnel Management Act and the Reserve Officer Personnel Management Act for laterally hiring civilian talent as military officers.

Interviewees spent relatively less time discussing training. Some interviewees noted that better training programs were necessary to build AI talent and technical abilities. However, there was uncertainty in how the services could create, offer, and scale these programs. Another open question was the role of contractors in providing the training. Some opportunities for officers to learn technical skills, though not specific to AI, already exist through education programs and rotations. For example, the Navy's Fleet Scholar Education Program partnered with CMU to create an in-residence cyber research program for officers. Kessel Run, a coding unit within the Air Force, partners airmen with industry partners to solve challenges related to automating processes for the Air Combat Command. The Air Force also offers a broader "Education with Industry Program" for servicemembers and civilians across a range of occupational specialties, including cyber.[8] To encourage permeability from the civilian side, the Marines created a new program in 2019 to access civilian cyber talent. The Cyber Auxiliary ("Cyber Aux") will enable volunteers to assist the Marines in providing and building the service's cyber capabilities without having to go through traditional training.[9] One interviewee expressed the opinion that DoD should cut down on National Defense University slots to send more people to industry for training.

When discussing training, some interviewees also raised the need to increase management awareness of AI and its abilities. These interviewees believed that although there was great momentum to integrate AI into existing operations from the top and bottom levels, middle management was a barrier.

---

[8] Air Force Institute of Technology, "AFIT Civilian Institution Programs," webpage, undated.

[9] Gina Harkins, "Marine Commandant: You Can Have Purple Hair in Our New Cyber Force," *Military.com*, April 29, 2019.

Insights from Interviews with Industry and Academia

In this appendix, we summarize the insights gleaned from our interviews in academia and industry. Some of these insights are factual statements; others report on opinions expressed. In particular, we have aimed to highlight themes that recurred in multiple interviews among a particular group (industry or academia): Although the fact that multiple people hold an opinion does not necessarily make it correct, we believe a theme's recurrence is worth pointing out. With few exceptions, we did not attempt to capture the prevalence of an opinion, instead using the word "some" to indicate a theme present across several interviews. Where we do report prevalence, we have attempted to clarify the relevant sample size. We also highlighted facts or opinions that, although not prevalent, we deemed important for offering an interesting perspective or a creative approach that might be valuable.

We chose to structure this appendix by separating the insights of academia from those of industry, owing to the starkly different missions and working environments. Within each category, we have organized these insights along the six dimensions of our posture assessment. We end the appendix by summarizing industry and academic opinions on regulation of AI, the potential for DoD to compete for AI talent, and the JAIC.

Industry

Organization

One of the topics we were eager to explore with our industry interviewees was how other organizations have scaled AI and the lessons learned therein. As expected, we heard a variety of experiences because of the substantially different natures of the companies we interviewed.[1] Nonetheless, we can extract certain common threads.

First, AI transformation, where it has happened, was mandated and orchestrated from the top down.

Second, the path to transformation typically involved setting up a centralized core team.

Third, AI transformation requires a long-term institutional commitment, including funding commitments and broad based support at the highest levels of the organization and across the executive team.[2]

We note here that the change management literature supports the need for mandates and broad-based support from top leadership to facilitate change in numerous ways, notably by overcoming risk aversion and enabling the organization to make mutually supportive changes in other areas, such as governance structures or strategies.[3]

Our interviewees noted the importance of developing a five-year strategic road map in executing this transformation and of defining an objective that is specific enough to inform the development of this strategic road map. Within this road map, they highlighted the importance of defining one-year goals and metrics to drive progress while

---

[1] We expect the path to transformation to be different for a technology company and for a nontechnology company, and there is a variety of options in between.

[2] On the subject of executive support, there was divergence of opinions. Some interviewed noted that transformation is most successful when the core team reports directly to the chief executive officer, and other interviewees noted that the success is more a function of the leader and how visionary that individual is rather than the leader's specific role on the executive team.

[3] John P. Kotter, "Leading Change: Why Transformation Efforts Fail," *Harvard Business Review*, May–June 1995; Roger Gill, "Change Management—or Change Leadership?" *Journal of Change Management*, Vol. 3, No. 4, 2002; Christian Matt, Thomas Hess, and Alexander Benlian, "Digital Transformation Strategies," *Business and Information Systems Engineering*, Vol. 57, No. 5, 2015.

simultaneously maintaining agility to redirect. They also highlighted the importance of concurrently considering infrastructure, talent, and workforce development. One of the interviewees highlighted two perspectives for strategy development, the first being a portfolio-based approach (the present, middle, and long terms) and the second being a domain-based approach, in which use cases are used to build up domains. The interviewee commented that the latter approach has advantages where building talent and aggregating data sets are concerned.

Ultimately, the solutions are not expected to remain static, and if the transformation is successful, AI should become embedded and decentralized in every part of the organization. However, centralization and visibility are important at the outset, according to our interviewees. One of our interviewees opined that decentralizing too early might inhibit success. And throughout the transformation process, there is a need for communicating value in a transparent way to ensure continued support from leadership. In that context, use cases offer a potential mechanism for doing just that.

It is worth noting here that some of the organizations we interviewed at already had diffuse capabilities in AI across the organization prior to establishing a centralized core team. In these cases, the motivations for setting up a centralized team appeared to be a combination of the desires to mount an organized response, establish a repository of internal knowledge, avoid duplication of efforts across the organization, and ensure a degree of external visibility to aid in attracting AI talent.

Another question we were eager to explore was that of typical failure modes for AI transformation at scale. We learned from our interviews that there are a variety of reasons for failure, including a lack of vision to tie the activities together, the launch of what were described as "pet projects" that did not connect well to the vision for AI and that were hard to scale, the lack of sufficient investment in supporting infrastructure, and viewing this endeavor as a one-time project rather than one requiring long-term commitment. In particular, it is important to have use cases to demonstrate utility and capture value, but it is also important that these test cases be tied to a longer term vision within a cohesive strategy.

Finally, we wanted to understand how the commercial world measures success, or alternatively, added value. Not surprisingly, return on investment, cost savings, increased revenue, and new business were all cited as measures of success. Two interviewees noted that having a baseline for comparison is important; for example, to claim that a process is now better, faster, or cheaper, you need to have a benchmark. One interviewee cited the measure of adoption as a potential metric.

Advancement and Adoption

One of our interviewees offered an interesting perspective on the difference between AI projects in academia and those in industry. In academia, a typical starting point is a given data set and a well-defined question or problem. The challenge is then to find a solution that is good enough.[4] In industry, the data set might not be fixed,[5] and translating the mission objective into a technical goal might not be straightforward. This perspective emphasizes the importance of focusing investments on transitioning basic research, a theme we will highlight again in this appendix when discussing insights from academia. This perspective also emphasizes the need for a spiral R&D approach for AI.

Regarding spiral R&D, one of our interviewees highlighted the importance of deploying AI solutions, even if they fail, to give the algorithms an opportunity to learn—with the caveat that one should begin with low-risk applications. Another interviewee highlighted the importance of bringing the technologists and users together, as part of an integrated team, to ensure that the technologist understands the problem requiring an AI solution, and to ensure that the user is comfortable with the AI solution when it is ready.[6] Several interviewees emphasized

---

[4] *Good enough* in an academic setting is often judged by whether it is publishable.

[5] There might be multiple data sets that could potentially be used, or data might be continuously collected.

[6] On that note, three interviewees highlighted the probabilistic nature of AI, and the need to get users and operators comfortable with that.

the need to start from the problem, or from a specific pain point, and work back toward a solution and the ecosystem around it.

The subject of open versus closed research came up in a couple of our interviews. The sense was that it generally pays to be open, particularly early on in the technology development.

On the subject of technology transfer, in this case from companies to clients, some interviewees highlighted that deploying AI solutions at scale is difficult, as the tools typically need to be integrated and customized to the users. Interviewees emphasized the need to allocate enough people and resources to enable the transition. We note that this appears to be supported by the literature, which advocates budgeting as much for integration as for technology.[7]

One aspect of commercially available solutions that came up in some of our interviews was that companies providing an AI solution are often unable to share details of how their algorithm arrived at its result because of intellectual property concerns. That lack of context sometimes limits users' ability to effectively use the AI solution to take action.

On the question of how companies decided whether to develop an AI technology in-house,[8] we learned the following: First, companies prefer to build in-house when they believe the product provides a strategic competitive advantage. One interviewee noted that whether they believe they will have a secure intellectual property position also contributes to that decision. Second, when acquiring companies, there are integration and acquisition costs, and both need to be taken into account in making the decision to acquire.

As expected, our industry interviewees also provided relevant insights on the current state of AI. We combined these with insights garnered from technical interviewees in academia, DoD, and other federal government agencies and our team's technical expertise and

---

[7]   Tim Fountaine, Brian McCarthy, and Tamim Saleh, "Building the AI-Powered Organization," *Harvard Business Review*, July–August 2019.

[8]   The term *in-house* refers to using in-house talent. The alternative options are to purchase the AI solution commercially off the shelf; to outsource a build; or, sometimes, to acquire the company that builds it.

review of the technical literature to render the assessment presented in Chapter Three. Therefore—and because these insights do not apply specifically to industry but to AI in general—we will not describe them here. In particular, the subject of VVT&E, including that of the data sets, came up in some of our industry interviews. When it did, the consensus was, unsurprisingly, that it was a difficult problem and one that was very important, especially for safety-critical systems. The trend appears to be the development of engineering best practices, individually and within industry consortia.[9]

We noted that the amount of investment in basic AI research within industry appears to be small, judging by the apparent lack of basic research groups in most of the organizations we interviewed, and by group size (in number of people) relative to the organization when such groups do exist.[10]

Finally, we gleaned insights from our interviews on the broad variety of current uses of AI in industry. These include robotic process automation to eliminate rote tasks, PM, demand forecasting, yield management, workforce planning to optimize worker efficiency in factories, human resources analytics, predictive models for human resources,[11] electronic trading, classification and routing of email, digital marketing, generating regulatory reports; assisting humans in reading long documents, computer vision in radiology and X-rays, and autonomous vehicles.

---

[9]   See, for example, the recent ABOUT ML initiative of the Partnership on AI (Partnership on AI, "About ML: Annotation and Benchmarking on Understanding and Transparency of Machine Learning Lifecycles," webpage, undated).

[10]   We consulted public records (10-K financial performance filings) of large companies with significant AI presence to get a sense of R&D investments. For 2018, these records indicate that Microsoft's R&D investments totaled $14.7 billion, with total revenue of $110.3 billion and total expenses of $35 billion; IBM's R&D investments totaled $5.3 billion, with total revenue of $79.5 billion and total expenses of $67.3 billion; and Alphabet's R&D investments totaled $21.4 billion, with total revenue of $136.8 billion and total expenses of $110.4 billion. It is not possible to determine from the public records the proportion of these R&D investments focusing on AI or basic research.

[11]   One such example is a model that predicts which employees are likely to leave next.

Innovation

Several of our interviewees highlighted the creation and (external) sharing of data sets as a successful means of spurring innovation.[12] A couple of the interviewees presented evidence of that success by noting publications, follow-up studies, and ensuing partnerships. On a related note, some of our interviewees with a history of working for DoD also highlighted the difficulty of securing access to DoD data as an impediment to innovation.

On developing an internal culture of innovation, interviewees cited the importance of giving a voice to lower-level employees and providing small amounts of paid time for passion projects related to those employees' products. Interviewees also highlighted the importance of creating a culture that tolerates failures as long as lessons are learned. In such a culture, failure should not threaten job security. Interviewees also highlighted the benefits of promoting a culture of openness and sharing through internal conferences and workshops. Participation in these efforts was incentivized by upper management; advances made as a result of employees' participation (e.g., transitioning the technology from a research unit to a product line) were rewarded. One interviewee discussed the role of an internal networking platform that allowed staff to voluntarily share details of their skills, experience, and interest in facilitating this culture of openness and sharing.

Interviewees from some organizations described the standing up of small, risk-taking organizations as separate units tangential to other aspects of the company, which allowed those organizations to isolate the risks from the larger organization. However, this deliberate separation had its downsides as well, leading to obstacles in technology transfer from innovation units to engineering units.

Other interviewees noted the importance of standing up entities responsible for engaging startups, offering access to engineers, technology, funding, and mentorship in exchange for intellectual property rights. Another interviewee noted that they had established facilitated

---

[12] Creating or curating a data set takes a lot of effort and provides little reward in terms of ability to publish. Providing free access to one is thus an enticing proposition for AI researchers.

pathways for contracting with academics and startups by minimizing paperwork and legal costs.

Data

Industry interviewees noted that a critical factor in successfully implementing and deploying effective AI algorithms was having access to large volumes of high-quality data. Yet across the spectrum, interviewees cited challenges with data, including difficulty collecting the needed data, difficulty accessing data that are siloed internally, difficulty accessing data on vendor platforms, difficulty accessing data stored across different platforms lacking interoperability, and the lack of standards and processes that would allow one to manage data and data pipelines in a manner consistent with their use for AI.

The organizations we interviewed represented a wide spectrum in terms of volumes and types of data they had available: Some had ample data, including historical data going back a decade or more. Others lacked sufficient data for envisioned ML approaches and cited difficulties collecting the data. Others had ample amounts of data, but a significant portion of the data was unstructured, rendering the data more difficult to leverage. One interviewee observed that moving from paper to digital offers an opportunity to redesign the data-capture process for the better, an opportunity that is not always taken. This observation highlights the need to evolve processes to best leverage new technologies, a recurring theme in our interviews.

Some interviewees struggled with legacy software applications whose data had not been designed for interoperability with data collected by other applications. Again, they mentioned that there were no simple solutions to this problem; engineers must either rewrite and modernize an application itself or write code to transform the application's data into a new form that can interoperate with other data sources. Interestingly, one of our interviewees expressed the opinion that the data diversity problem might be better solved by humans communicating rather than mandating standardized processes. None of the interviewees described a centralized solution that had alleviated their difficulties.

Some interviewees believed that data quality was the most important factor in whether an AI project would ultimately be successful. Nonetheless, several interviewees noted difficulties with data quality and highlighted the critical importance of data engineering, echoing our academic interviewees. Interviewees also described the immense amounts of work needed to curate data and ensure the data stayed clean over time. None described any shortcut to improving data quality; each data set needed engineers to look for issues, investigate root causes, and implement improvements to ensure the data collected accurately reflected the real-world conditions.

Not all of the industry participants indicated having a storage and computing infrastructure adequate for current needs to prototype with or implement AI-based applications. Some credited the development of cloud computing and the availability of cloud storage for the ability to retain the ever-increasing amounts of data stored by their software applications.

Our industry interviewees described struggles sharing data because of privacy rules. Additionally, several interviewees noted constraints because of regulations that require geolocating data storage within the country of collection. On that note, one of our interviewees mentioned that there has been more interest in distributed learning in conjunction with the use of federated networks that maintain data locally while providing access to the network remotely, possibly from other countries. Some of our interviewees expressed concerns about maintaining data rights, particularly in the context of use with commercial vendor platforms, and mentioned the potential for disputes over data ownership.

Finally, our interviews showed the difficulties that many organizations face in transforming their culture to become more data-centric. One interviewee observed that too often, initiatives to scale AI are thought of as simply an IT project, when, in reality, they require a greater scope of change throughout the organization, including engaging the entire workforce to gain acceptance for this organizational transformation and truly understanding the workflows and day-to-day operations of the organization.

Talent

All our industry interviewees were unanimous in stating that AI talent is difficult to find, hire, and retain. The turnover rates they cited varied from two to four years. The demand for AI talent varied across the interviewees we spoke with, depending on their companies' business models. Interviewees discussed a differentiation between in-house AI development and contracting out, which inherently affects the size and scope of an organization's internal AI workforce.

On the types of AI talent, our takeaway was that were several broad categories of talent are needed to enable the development, production, and management of AI products: Ph.D.-level expert practitioners, ML developers, application developers, and product or project managers. Interviewees indicated shortages in all categories of talent. Several interviewees also noted that software engineers, computer scientists, and data scientists with explicit training in AI or ML were among the most sought-after skills.

Interviewees mentioned several ways of accessing AI talent in addition to traditional hiring and recruiting processes. First, some interviewees highlighted the importance of networks and personal connections. Second, some interviewees emphasized the creation of organizational initiatives that establish university pipelines to enhance recruiting, with several of the organizations having established formal partnerships. These included research partnerships, joint appointments for faculty and staff, consulting opportunities, internship opportunities, and sponsorship of Ph.D. students working alongside employees on projects. Third, some interviewees noted obtaining talent by acquisition of smaller AI start-ups.[13]

---

[13] This appears to be a strategy employed across industries, whether the company is a native AI or technology company or a legacy firm building AI capabilities to advance its product offerings. For example, in 2019 alone, McDonald's acquired two AI companies to enhance internal operations and customer experience. See Brian Barrett, "McDonald's Doubles Down on Tech with Voice AI Acquisition," *Wired*, September 10, 2019. S&P Global acquired an AI start-up in 2019 to assist in predictive analytics; see Ron Miller, "S&P Global Snares Kensho for $550 Million," TechCrunch, March 7, 2018. Data suggest that technology firms are leading AI through acquisition, particularly for talent, with Apple, Google, Microsoft, Facebook, and Amazon among the top companies. See "The Race for AI: Here Are the Tech

Some of the interviewees stated that they had open publication policies to enhance retention of talent coming from academia. One of the interviewees noted that access to proprietary data sets can be used as a recruitment tool. Some interviewees also noted that internal competitions can cross-fertilize ideas and bring together an AI-minded community. These and other internal efforts also allowed for voluntary skill cataloging, creating a repository of available skills within the company.

The subject of training came up in some our interviews. Sometimes, internal courses were used to train technical talent in AI: The motivation was either to cover AI talent shortages or to get (other) domain experts up to speed on AI. Some companies offered voluntary intensive CS and coding courses to upskill their employees, with several offering publicly available courses and certifications that are AI-related. Some interviewees also cited the need for internal training to educate senior leadership on the basics of AI.

Academia

Organization

One of the broad themes we wanted to explore in our academic interviews was that of measures of success. We heard the following viewpoint, which applies in particular to AI but is not AI-specific: Success in building partnerships among entities or organizations can be measured in terms of increased return relationships. Transactional engagements (e.g., a collaborative project) are needed to build trust, but the goal is to build toward strategic engagements that go beyond the transactional.

Advancement and Adoption

A recurrent theme in our academic interviews was the inter- and intra-disciplinary nature of AI research. Several interviewees highlighted the importance of overcoming cultural barriers and pursuing interdisci-

---

Giants Rushing to Snap Up Artificial Intelligence Startups," CBInsights, webpage, September 17, 2019.

plinary approaches to advance AI. Interviewees also highlighted the wide impact of AI and its applications across all disciplines, including medicine and law. Finally, interviewees highlighted that cross-disciplinary endeavors are important for identifying new basic research problems and inspiring new research directions.

A second theme in our interviews was that it is difficult to develop good metrics to measure the progress or success of basic research.[14]

We highlight two academic perspectives on the topic of technology transfer from academia to industry. One of our interviewees noted the importance of demonstrating a prototype at a reasonable scale, and the importance of understanding industry problems and bottlenecks through close sustained interactions with industry for successful technology transfer. This view underscores the importance of building stable relationships. Another interviewee highlighted the importance of devoting significant resources to technology transfer, rather than treating it as an afterthought of R&D, and commented that the team that does technology transfer should probably be bigger than the team that develops the initial idea.[15]

As expected, our academic interviewees who were technical (seven out of the ten interviewees) also provided relevant insights on the current state of AI. We combined these with insights garnered from technical interviewees in industry, DoD, and other federal government agencies and our team's technical expertise and review of the technical literature to render the assessment presented in Chapter Three. Because they do not apply specifically to academia but to AI in general, we will not describe them here. However, we will note that five of the seven technical interviewees highlighted VVT&E of ML systems as an area of concern, with two elaborating further on concerns about lack of robustness and quantification uncertainty.

---

[14] We heard similar comments on the difficulty of developing good metrics from our interviews at DoD research labs and basic research organizations. It is unclear whether the implication is that measuring progress in applied research is easier.

[15] Although we were unable to verify the specific comment about team size, this general opinion resonates with some of our industry interviews that similarly highlighted the importance of devoting significant, continuing resources toward technology transfer and adoption at scale.

Finally, we note that interviewees at all the academic organizations mentioned relationships and ongoing work with the basic research arms of DoD (DARPA, the Air Force Office of Scientific Research, the Office of Naval Research, and ARL). Only four of our nine interviewees mentioned the JAIC and appeared to be aware of it.

Data

On the subject of data, several of our interviewees brought up struggles with data sharing and data governance because of institutional review board and privacy concerns.[16] Some interviewees opined that these struggles were impeding AI research and adoption in health care, although one interviewee noted that DoD has a gold mine of longitudinal health care data that are unavailable elsewhere.

Another emerging theme was the importance of data engineering,[17] the lack of support for data engineers in academic grants, and the need for proper documentation of processes and data sets, particularly when there is turnover in project staff.

Chief among the concerns brought up in our interviews is the lack of adequate computing infrastructure at academic institutions and the significant relative advantage that industry holds in that domain. Although the interviewees expressing these concerns all had access to cloud computing, several pointed out that reliance on that alone is problematic for a variety of reasons, such as prohibitive cost to projects, difficulty customizing, and issues encountered in prototyping and deployment of AI approaches.[18] Some interviewees articulated the need for more funding for computing resources and for pursuing a mix of cloud-based and institutional cluster-based capabilities. On the posi-

---

[16] An institutional review board is an appropriately constituted group that is formally designated to review and monitor biomedical research involving human subjects, and that, under Food and Drug Administration regulations, has the authority to approve or disapprove research, or to require research modifications to secure approval.

[17] *Data engineering* includes the building of pipelines to collect data and the curation and preparation of the data sets collected for research or analysis purposes.

[18] It is important to emphasize that these concerns about cloud computing were strictly from the academic perspective. We caution against extrapolating it beyond academia. Indeed, we did not hear similar comments echoed by our industry interviewees.

tive side, one interviewee speculated that the need for large common computational infrastructure and the push for shared resources might lead to a breakdown of the data barriers.

Talent

The difficulty that even top academic institutions are having in retaining AI talent (faculty and research staff) was a recurring theme. Typically, this phenomenon was viewed as a major cause for concern, potentially slowing down fundamental progress or leading to shortages in faculty to train the next generation of researchers. However, faculty and researcher engagement in commercial companies was looked upon favorably in one of the academic institutions represented. That was not entirely surprising to the team, as we noticed while planning for our academic interviews that many prominent AI faculty have, or have had, commercial affiliations as well. This phenomenon and its apparent effects on innovation were the subject of a recent academic study.[19]

The overall sense was that academic institutions cannot compete with industry on salaries but can provide other retention incentives, primarily flexibility and access. Examples of such incentives include allowing faculty to take multiyear industry sabbaticals and then return to their faculty roles; allowing faculty more consulting time or half-time appointments;[20] providing research staff with lots of autonomy, including the ability to change managers or research groups; providing research staff with flexible career paths and opportunities to move into and out of roles; and providing faculty and research staff with access to interesting data sets.

A corollary of that theme is the perception—alluded to in a couple of the interviews and implicit in industry's desire to hire the top AI faculty—that an excellent AI researcher might be worth much more, from a technical perspective, than would several average researchers,

---

[19] Michael Gofman and Zhao Jin, "Artificial Intelligence, Human Capital, and Innovation," University of Rochester, working paper, August 20, 2019.

[20] The current prevalent model for consulting time is to allow faculty one day per week for external consulting activities, generally considered to account for 20 percent of their weekly effort.

and that hiring a top researcher also allows companies to tap into that person's network of students and collaborators.

Thoughts Across Industry and Academia

We end this appendix by summarizing interviewee thoughts, from both industry and academia, on two important topics: the regulation of AI and how DoD can better compete for AI talent.

On the Regulation of AI

Although the subject of regulation of AI was not a focus of our academic or industry interviews, it did come up in our meetings, sometimes in response to questions we posed and at other times unprompted. We heard a variety of thoughts on the subject that we summarize here.

The opinions expressed on regulation were nuanced. Some of the interviewees called for the establishment of regulations on the use of AI, primarily out of fear of a big disaster negatively affecting continued research and progress.[21] Others expressed the concern that too much regulation would stifle innovation. One interviewee mused that although no individual regulation would be concerning, collectively, several uncoordinated regulations might become problematic. Others expressed the fear that regulations might not be able to keep up with the fast pace of technology, or that there would be a tendency to over-regulate before the technology is well understood. Data rights, and in particular the new European Union General Data Protection Regulation, came up in several meetings. Industry appears to be watching to see how this regulation affects European competitiveness in AI. Finally, several interviewees expressed the opinion that it might behoove industry to self-regulate.[22]

---

[21] We note here that there is a difference between regulating AI *use* and regulating AI *development*.

[22] The founding in September 2016 of the Partnership on AI, a technology industry consortium, might herald a move in the direction of self-regulation.

One message that we heard in both academic and industry interviews was the need for the United States to maintain its position as a magnet for AI talent worldwide.

On DoD Competing for AI Talent

We also summarize interviewee thoughts, mostly unprompted, about how DoD can enhance its access to AI talent. The views we heard expressed in industry and academia were remarkably similar, summarized in three key messages.

First, emphasis on the mission is the way for DoD to attract AI talent.[23]

Second, AI talent is attracted to challenging technical problems, which DoD has in spades.

Third, DoD might find that releasing interesting data sets attracts partnerships, because talent gravitates toward data.

On the JAIC

Although the JAIC was not a specific subject of discussion with our industry and academic interviewees, it nonetheless came up in some of our interviews. We collect here the thoughts and impressions we heard about the JAIC.

Three industry interviewees familiar with the JAIC weighed in. One interviewee noted that DoD messaging is confusing to external observers. On the one hand, the JAIC has been touted as the face of DoD AI; on the other hand, money is a source of power within DoD, and the lack of budget authorities—or even a significant budget—presents a starkly conflicting message. A second interviewee noted that it is unclear how the JAIC will be able to pull together use cases, labeled data sets, performance metrics, and baselines to demonstrate value in scaling AI. A third interviewee noted that there might be an opportunity for the JAIC to build AI talent and AI solutions in-house, with the implication that this might be an advisable course.

---

[23] Several interviewees noted the importance of communicating the mission well, and proactively.

Insights from Historical Case Studies

In this appendix, we provide a brief overview of the six historical case studies considered and highlight insights gleaned from each of them that might be relevant to our study. As we discussed in Appendix A, we did not seek to compare or contrast insights across case studies, in view of their markedly distinct natures.

AI History in DoD

Amid the excitement and hype, it is perhaps easy to forget that AI, and DoD involvement in it, are far from new.[1] Our first case study examined the history of AI in DoD, which parallels the history of AI itself, as DoD was the primary funder of AI and ML throughout the second half of the 20th century.[2]

Funding for AI and ML research in the 1950s came primarily from DoD, with modest contributions from private foundations (e.g., the Rockefeller Foundation) and industry (e.g., IBM). When IBM support of AI research suddenly stopped at the beginning of the 1960s, the Advanced Research Projects Agency (ARPA) emerged as the primary DoD funder of AI research. In that era, ARPA funded

---

[1] The research for this case study drew upon 31 sources from the literature. Of those, we only reference here those sources that support the narrative leading up to the relevant insights.

[2] National Research Council, *Funding a Revolution: Government Support for Computing Research*, Washington, D.C.: The National Academy Press, 1999.

"people, not projects," and deliverables were either poorly specified or not expected at all. Considerable DoD-funded AI research programs were also maintained at think tanks, such as the RAND Corporation and the Stanford Research Institute. Changes both outside and inside ARPA compelled a major shift in DoD funding from basic AI research toward direct military applications during the 1970s.[3] Unmet expectations, and sometimes the lack of well-specified performance criteria, stoked much of the disappointment inside and outside ARPA with progress in AI research and led to reductions of research funding for years to follow.[4] For example, the 1966 Automatic Language Processing Advisory Committee report found that machine language translation research up to that time, such as the Mark II Automatic Language Translator at Wright-Patterson Air Force Base, had failed to achieve its goals of improving the accuracy, speed, or cost-effectiveness of human translators.[5] As another example, the 1970s Speech Understanding Program, which sought a speech recognition system that could attain a ten-thousand-word vocabulary with an arbitrary speaker was funded as a five-year, $3 million program in 1971 with the expectation of a five-year follow-on. After the three completed systems were demonstrated in 1976, DARPA administrators and the AI researchers disagreed about whether the performance criteria had been met, as the testing procedure had not been fully specified at the beginning of the project.[6]

At the beginning of the 1980s, it appeared to many that the moment had arrived for AI to transition to practical applications for

---

[3] The 1969 Mansfield amendment, which forbade DoD from funding basic research except for that with "direct and apparent" relevance for military applications, disallowed the kind of open-ended basic research funding that ARPA had provided to AI researchers in the 1960s (Public Law 91-121, An Act to Authorize Appropriations During the Fiscal Year 1970, Title II, Section 203, November 19, 1969).

[4] National Research Council, 1999; Daniel Crevier, *AI: The Tumultuous History of the Search for Artificial Intelligence*, New York: Basic Books, 1993.

[5] Automatic Language Processing Advisory Committee, *Language and Machines: Computers in Translation and Linguistics*, Washington, D.C.: National Academy of Sciences, National Research Council, Publication 1416, 1966.

[6] Crevier, 1993.

both the defense and civilian sectors.[7] In 1983, DARPA launched the Strategic Computing Program (SCP), whose objective was to provide "a broad base of machine intelligence technology for application to critical defense problems" by developing "a new generation of computers that can SEE, HEAR, TALK, PLAN, and REASON."[8] SCP was an experiment with an unprecedented and ambitious new funding model that sought to address pressures from inside and outside DoD, opposing the way DARPA had funded its researchers over the previous two decades.[9] SCP attempted to circumvent this pressure by conducting basic technology development as part of applied research oriented toward specific projects tailored for different armed services. It succeeded in greatly increasing the amount of R&D funding devoted to AI and advanced computing and in cultivating a greater pool of AI talent. But it soon became apparent that the technical goals laid out in 1983 were far too ambitious and that some of the hoped-for applications could not be developed with available technology, much less transitioned to operational use.

The mid-1980s also witnessed the thaw of the long "neural net winter," which started in the 1960s, that came about because of increased processing power that made it practical to simulate neural networks on conventional computers. Around the beginning of 1987, commercial investors turned sour on AI—it would take a bit longer for DoD to sour as well. Indeed, DARPA announced the Artificial Neural Network Technology Program in December 1988. The program had a $33 million dollar budget for a 28-month exploratory seed program to investigate the new technology. Nonetheless, expert systems were turning out to be far less than the game-changer promised, often costing more to develop and maintain than the humans they replaced. Com-

---

[7] Ingvar Åkersten, "The Strategic Computing Program," in Allan M. Din, ed., *Arms and Artificial Intelligence: Weapon and Arms Control Applications of Advanced Computing*, New York: Oxford University Press, 1987, p. 86

[8] Åkersten, 1987, p. 87.

[9] Skeptics in both Congress and DoD disapproved of the open-ended funding for exploratory basic research that had been provided to the AI research centers, instead pushing for applied research connected to concrete military applications.

mercial disillusionment deflated the nascent AI industry, resulting in the most notorious "AI winter." After a few years, neural networks lost their luster as well because it was only practical to train relatively shallow neural networks on available computers leading to modest empirical successes. The academic researchers who persevered to realize the promise of DL we are witnessing today sometimes called this period a second "neural net winter." Yann LeCun, the 2018 A. M. Turing prize winner for contributions to the computing field co-awardee, attributed the second "neural net winter" to an aesthetic preference for theoretical tractability among ML researchers. LeCun expressed concern that overhyping DL "could easily lead to another 'winter cycle.'"[10]

In summary, the insights gleaned from this case study that potentially align with our dimensions of posture assessment are as follows:

- **Organization, Advancement, Adoption:** The history of AI is rife with mismanaged expectations and premature hype. We should be careful not to repeat that history.
- **Advancement, Adoption:** A corollary to that is that DoD should resist the temptation to try to force technological progress by scheduling the transition of immature technologies as the SCP attempted to do.
- **Organization, Advancement:** It was and remains difficult even for experts to predict which tasks will prove easy and which will prove hard.[11] Practical experience is always the final arbiter of difficulty. It is therefore important to maintain agility and flexibility and hedge against premature technological lock-in.

---

[10] Lee Gomes, "Facebook AI Director Yann LeCun on His Quest to Unleash Deep Learning and Make Machines Smarter," *IEEE Spectrum*, February 18, 2015.

[11] For instance, much of what was considered AI in the 1950s and 1960s is considered basic CS today. Such applications as machine language translation were misperceived as straightforward programming problems rather than challenging AI tasks.

History of Software Development in DoD

DoD software capabilities have been actively developing over the past 60 years, both for infrastructure and for defense weapon systems.[12] Given that a significant portion of the current AI technology is digitally implemented, DoD's posture for software affects that of AI, hence this case study.

Long ago, DoD had military standards for software procurement, development, and documentations that established "uniform minimum requirements for the development of software for the DoD."[13] Indeed, these standards introduced several layers of documentation—specifications and design, deliverables, and approval cycles—most of which were required upfront for project sign on. These and subsequent military software standards were canceled in the 1990s in lieu of using commercial standards and various forms of incremental software development. Even after the cancellation of the 2167A military standard on defense system software development,[14] the large volume of required documentation and review processes led to increased emphasis on tailoring in the 2015 revision of the Department of Defense Instruction (DoDI) 5000.02.[15] DoD continues to emphasize tailoring in its ongoing revision of DoD instructions and guidance.

Iterative and incremental development (such as Agile software development) goes back decades.[16] In 2001, the approach evolved into the Agile Methodology as an alternative to top-down development process and management, and its subsequent general adoption by the soft-

---

[12] The research for this case study drew upon 20 sources from the literature. Of those, we reference here only those sources that underpin the narrative leading up to the relevant insights.

[13] Department of Defense Standard 1679A, *Military Standard Software Development*, Washington, D.C., DOD-STD-1679, Revision A, 1983.

[14] Department of Defense Standard 2167A, *Defense System Software Development*, Washington, D.C., DOD-STD-2167A, February 29, 1988.

[15] Department of Defense Instruction 5000.02, *Operation of Defense Acquisition System*, Washington, D.C., January 7, 2015.

[16] See the review by Craig Larman and Victor R. Basili, "Iterative and Incremental Development: A Brief History," *Computer*, Vol. 36, No. 6, June 2003.

ware industry.[17] Agile development methods recognize the significant gap in perspectives between the software engineers who must implement computer programs, those that set the requirements for the software, and the workers who must ultimately use these applications in their day-to-day jobs. Consequently, Agile advocates for interactions among people over formalized processes and working software over up-front planning and documentation. Agile also advocates frequent feedback between teams and stakeholders after every incremental development, which allows the stakeholders to direct the software development team toward the functionality actually needed instead of what had been originally specified, avoiding rework/delays/additional costs and improving the ultimate utility of the final product. Even for cases in which DoD policies and projects have adopted iterative and Agile software by policy, some projects have failed to adopt the underlying tenets of Agile project development and have continued to follow waterfall procedures under a different terminology. Agile is not appropriate for every software development, but it is seen as a major approach for many applications to speed development through user-informed requirements adjustment and satisficing.

A notable point in DoD software history was the establishment, in 1984, of the Software Engineering Institute, an FFRDC. This development was a response to DoD's realization that software technology was becoming an enabler for flexibility and integration in mission-critical systems, that software was often a cause of system delays and failures, and that there was a need to have an organization of software engineers and software researchers familiar with DoD-related problems who were available to assist.[18] The Software Engineering Institute developed a capability maturity model (CMM and Capability Maturity Model Integration [CMMI]) primarily for DoD (although it later became an international standard, with other federal agencies, commer-

---

[17] "Manifesto for Agile Software Development," webpage, undated.

[18] Larry Druffel, *A Technical History of the SEI*, Pittsburgh, Pa.: Carnegie Mellon University, CMU/SEI-2016-SR-027, January 2017.

cial industry, and governments enforcing the CMMI requirements).[19] The focus of this CMM was to create a single framework that organizations could use for enterprisewide process improvement initiatives. CMM and CMMI levels have since proven to have many limitations, including cumbersome processes, cost (in terms of time and effort), and lack of applicability to smaller organizations (effectively removing them from bidding). Ultimately, CMMI-level certification did not guarantee project success.[20] In 2007, DoD removed the CMMI-level requirement, preferring to use it only as a process improvement role.

In 2003, the Joint Capabilities Integration and Development System (JCIDS) was established as the primary means for the JROC (the Joint Requirements Oversight Council) to fulfill its statutory responsibilities of validating joint warfighting requirements. JROC is one of three parts of the overall DoD decision support system, which includes the PPBE process, JCIDS, and the Defense Acquisition System. The JCIDS requirements process is upfront and often long, with the system effectively functioning on a requirements pull rather than a requirements push methodology.[21]

The DIB's 2019 SWAP study recommended replacing the JCIDS, PPBE process, and Defense Federal Acquisition Regulation Supplement with a portfolio management approach to software programs.[22] In July 2019, DoD drafted a new Software Acquisition Pathway Policy[23] which was part of the DoD rewriting of DoDI 5000.02, creating a

---

[19] Software Engineering Institute, "Brief History of CMMI," Carnegie Mellon University, 2009.

[20] Saja A. Albliwi, Jiju Antony, and Norin Arshed, "Critical Literature Review on Maturity Models for Business Process Excellence," *2014 IEEE International Conference on Industrial Engineering and Engineering Management*, 2015.

[21] Joint Chiefs of Staff, *Charter of the Joint Requirements Oversight Council (JROC) and Implementation of the Joint Capabilities Integration and Development System (JCIDS)*, Washington, D.C., CJCSI 5123.01H, August 31, 2018; Section 809 Panel, *Report of the Advisory Panel on Streamlining and Codifying Acquisition Regulations*, Vol. 2, June 2018.

[22] Defense Innovation Board, 2019b.

[23] This policy is still in draft form as policymakers are considering the recommendations of the SWAP study (U.S. Department of Defense, *Software Acquisition Pathway Policy*, predecisional draft, Washington, D.C., undated, Not available to the general public).

new pathway and instruction for software acquisition.[24] The primary points of the pathway, which proposes two phases—planning and execution—are the definition and development of a minimum viable product (MVP) and a minimum viable capability release (MVCR).[25] It also proposes the establishment of iterative software methodologies, such as Agile, Lean and/or SecDevOps (in accordance with the recommendation of the DoD SWAP 2019 study).

In summary, the insights gleaned from this case study that potentially align with our dimensions of posture assessment are as follows:

- **Advancement and Adoption:** The prior history of DoD with software is one of cautionary tales about fixating on processes and standards at the expense of productivity and delivery.
- **Advancement and Adoption:** This case study also points to the challenges in aligning current best practices in industry and the current state of software in DoD.

Without further progress, these issues will negatively affect DoD's ability to scale all digital technologies, including AI, and thus they need to be further addressed without delay.

DoD Posture for Cyber

The 2018 NDS describes cyber as a foundational capability for the joint force.[26] Cyberspace capabilities are digital technologies that are

---

[24] National Defense Industrial Association, "DoD Rewrite of 5000 Series to Include a Software Acquisition Pathway," webpage, July 26, 2019.

[25] The MVP is an early iteration of a software project that has just enough features to meet basic minimum functional capabilities. The goal of an MVP is to quickly get basic capabilities into users' hands for evaluation, feedback, and improvements. The MVCR is a small set of features that provides value and capability to the Warfighter or end user and is intended to reduce deployment time (U.S. Department of Defense, undated, Not available to the general public).

[26] U.S. Department of Defense, 2018d, p. 7.

pervasive across DoD and that require specialized technical talent.[27] Because of this, a case study on DoD's posture for cyber might provide interesting insights that could be extrapolated to AI. We focus in particular on the talent aspect in this section.

Concerns about DoD posture for cyber date back to at least 1970. In that year, the Defense Science Board Computer Security Task Force issued a report that concluded immediate action was needed and suggested two approaches to task a government agency.[28] No such agency was created in the years following. Eventually, in 2009, Secretary of Defense Robert M. Gates established U.S. Cyber Command as a subcommand under U.S. Strategic Command.[29]

The National Military Strategy of 2004 declared cyberspace as a separate warfighting domain.[30] The first U.S. cyber strategy was published in 2011,[31] and in 2018, the United States released its second cyber strategy.[32] Today, the DoD CIO's roles have expanded to information management, IT, cybersecurity, certification of the DoD IT budget, and development and enforcement of IT standards. The Defense Information Systems Agency, which operates under the direction of the DoD CIO, is a combat support agency that builds, operates, and secures IT infrastructure. The principal cyber advisor (PCA) is the civilian adviser to the Secretary of Defense on DoD military and civilian cyber forces and activities.[33]

---

[27] The research for this case study drew upon 51 sources from the literature. Of those, we only reference here those sources that support the narrative leading up to the relevant insights.

[28] U.S. Department of Defense, 2018d, p. vii.

[29] Robert M. Gates, *Duty: Memoirs of a Secretary at War*, New York: Vintage Books, 2014.

[30] Joint Chiefs of Staff, *The National Military Strategy of the United States of America: A Strategy for Today, a Vision for Tomorrow*, Washington, D.C.: U.S. Department of Defense, 2004.

[31] Barack Obama, *International Strategy for Cyberspace: Prosperity, Security, and Openness in a Networked World*, White House: Washington, D.C., May 2011.

[32] Trump, 2019.

[33] Dana Deasy, "On DoD Cybersecurity Policies and Architecture," statement before the Senate Armed Services Committee Subcommittee on Cyber Security, Washington, D.C.:

The DoD posture in cyber is still evolving and its effectiveness is not yet ascertained, but already it appears possible to gain potentially useful insights in the area of talent management. Cyber talent within DoD, as a distinct operational function area, is relatively new. The Federal Cybersecurity Workforce Assessment Act of 2015 instructed DoD to create a separate set of occupational specialty codes for uniformed servicemembers.[34] The result has been that each service subsequently introduced cyber-specific occupational codes, reclassifying servicemembers as appropriate. That said, each service has its own occupational classification system, and each system classifies cyber talent differently.

Similarly, classification of the civilian cyber workforce was mandated by the Cybersecurity Workforce Assessment Act of 2015, with the Office of Personnel Management (OPM) developing a cyber occupational classification coding structure that all federal agencies were instructed to use.[35] DoD's resulting Cyber Workforce Framework is split into four categories, each with its own functional community: (1) cybersecurity IT, (2) cybersecurity, (3) cyberspace effects, and (4) intelligence workforce (cyberspace).[36] The first two communities are managed by the DoD CIO, the third category is managed by DoD's PCA, and the fourth category is overseen by USD(I).

There was no clear leadership of cyber talent management in DoD's Cyber Strategy.[37] The result has been that no one focal point exists for cyber talent. Coordination among the four communities occurs through the Cyber Workforce Management Board, which has three separate chairs and many members. Cyber talent demand is ultimately categorized and determined by function and mission.

U.S. Senate, 2019.

[34] Public Law 114–113, Consolidated Appropriations Act, 2016, Title III, Federal Cybersecurity Workforce Assessment Act of 2015, December 18, 2015.

[35] William Newhouse, Stephanie Keith, Benjamin Scribner, and Greg Witter, *National Initiative for Cybersecurity Education (NICE) Cybersecurity Workforce Framework*, Gaithersburg, Md.: National Institute of Standards and Technology, U.S. Department of Commerce, NIST Special Publication 800–181, August 2017.

[36] U.S. Department of Defense, 2018d, p. 6.

[37] U.S. Department of Defense, 2018d, p. 6.

In summary, the insights gleaned from this case study that potentially align with our dimensions of posture assessment are as follows:

- **Talent:** The DoD cyber community continues to grapple with challenges in recruiting and retaining top talent. Recent pay, compensation, and hiring flexibilities have been instituted for cyber, with much of the legal phrasing broad enough to include all emerging technologies.[38]
- **Talent:** As a cautionary tale, the classification systems for cyber talent took years of development, planning, and coordination across DoD, OPM, NIST, and other stakeholders. With cyber, DoD was limited in its ability to act in isolation from concurrent efforts in the executive and legislative branches; DoD had to work alongside OPM, even as DoD was already in the process of creating its own cyber workforce framework.[39]

Having said that, DoD continues to evolve its posture for cyber, and it is therefore unclear whether the current posture is adequate. This is a cautionary note for drawing conclusions from our study.

The Offset Strategy

This case study examined the history of the *offset strategy* that was pursued by Secretary of Defense Harold Brown and Undersecretary of Defense William Perry during the Carter administration.[40] Faced with Warsaw Pact numerical superiority and intractable political obstacles against matching this numerical superiority in kind, Brown and Perry needed a cost-effective alternative to deter possible Soviet aggression and assure allies. Recognizing the sizable lead enjoyed by

---

[38] Indeed, some of our DoD interviewees were already considering ways to leverage those flexibilities to hire AI talent in the absence of other clear mechanisms to do so.

[39] Pub. L. 114–113, Title III, 2015.

[40] The research for this case study drew upon 17 sources from the literature. Of those, we only reference here those sources that support the narrative leading up to the relevant insights.

the United States in computer and information technology, the offset strategy aimed to exploit that technology to provide the U.S. military with enhanced command, control, communications and intelligence (C3I); defense suppression (stealth) capability; and precision guidance.[41] Many observers credited the "offset" with enabling the spectacular U.S. victories over Iraq in 1991 and 2003. The offset strategy is often cited, most influentially by Bob Work in a much-quoted 2014 speech, as an example of how the United States has leveraged technology to overcome specific strategic and military challenges.[42] Because the "offset" resulted in fielded military systems, it offers a concrete example of how innovation can be shepherded through advancement and adoption. But not all of the technologies sought as part of the offset strategy reached fruition, and some of those that did proved disappointments on the battlefield. Comparing those technologies that became fielded capabilities with those that did not offers valuable lessons that could inform DoD's efforts to posture itself for AI.

Perry argued that it was a mistake to conceptualize the offset strategy as just an effort to make "better weapons" than those of the Soviets. Instead, "the offset strategy was based . . . on the premise that it was necessary to give these weapons a significant competitive advantage . . . by supporting them on the battlefield with newly developed equipment that multiplied their combat effectiveness"[43] and forced U.S. opponents to compete in technology areas where the U.S. was comparatively strong. Perry identified "three components of this support capability" that "were most critical to the remarkable success of coalition forces in the Gulf War."[44] These included defense suppression (particularly stealth), precision guidance, and C3I.[45] Notably, these were all foremost air capabilities whose implementation fell almost

---

[41] William J. Perry, "Desert Storm and Deterrence," *Foreign Affairs*, Vol. 70, No. 4, Fall 1991.

[42] Bob Work, speech delivered at convocation exercises at National Defense University, Washington, D.C., August 5, 2014.

[43] Perry, 1991.

[44] Perry, 1991.

[45] Perry, 1991.

entirely under the purview of a single service—the Air Force—and therefore did not have to contend with interservice rivalries.

But the technologies that contributed to victory over Saddam Hussein's Iraq were a mere fraction of those that DoD aspired to develop under the offset strategy. Although stealth aircraft and Global Positioning System (GPS) became linchpins of U.S. military capabilities, other components of Perry's strategy were less fruitful. For example, many of the systems envisioned to counter Soviet armor with precision conventional munitions under the aegis of the Assault Breaker initiative never reached fruition. The contrast between these outcomes is potentially instructive, offering insights into the difficulty of innovation and adoption for new military technologies. Latter-day accounts attribute the failure to actualize Assault Breaker to failures of interservice coordination, but unrealistic expectations, immature technology, and qualitative differences between ground and air combat all played a role.[46]

The F-117A stealth fighter and NAVSTAR GPS emerged from research efforts that were well underway by the mid-1970s and had already met proof-of-concept demonstrations.[47] These systems could also reach fruition without interservice coordination. Assault Breaker, by contrast, needed several undemonstrated technologies to become viable, and the cooperation of the Air Force and Army. The program languished without clear service ownership, and only a few of the envisioned components turned into fielded capabilities, most significantly the Joint Surveillance and Target Attack Radar System. But the radar

---

[46] Richard H. Van Atta, Alethia Cook, Ivars Gutmanis, Michael J. Lippitz, and Jasper Lupo, *Transformation and Transition: DARPA's Role in Fostering an Emerging Revolution in Military Affairs*, Vol. 2, *Detailed Assessments*, Alexandria, Va.: Institute for Defense Analyses, November 2003; Edward C. Keefer, *Harold Brown: Offsetting the Soviet Military Challenge, 1977–1981*, Washington, D.C.: Historical Office, Office of the Secretary of Defense, 2017, pp. 247–274.

[47] Even these programs were not unalloyed success stories. The F-117A was originally conceived as a stepping stone toward a stealth bomber that did not become a reality until the B-2 Spirit reached initial operational capability in 1997. In 1978, Brown approved the termination of the expensive and then-ineffective NAVSTAR GPS program, whose funding was then restored by Undersecretary Perry. Moreover, the Russian GLONASS program became operational only one year after NAVSTAR.

system itself came under criticism because of its questionable performance in Bosnia, an outcome that the GAO attributed to a lack of appropriate CONOPs at the time of its acquisition.[48] Several of the technologies envisioned for Assault Breaker would seriously test the state-of-the-art even today; the prospect that they could be operationalized within a few years and at a bargain price (Perry predicted in 1978 that Assault Breaker could be developed "in five years" and at a cost of just "a few billion dollars") was exceedingly overoptimistic.[49]

The offset strategy was a success, but it succeeded at something other than what it was originally intended to do. The systems developed as part of the offset strategy contributed to U.S. military supremacy in the 1990s and 2000s, but many of the capabilities Perry envisioned in the 1970s remained elusive.[50] The offset strategy succeeded to the extent that it did because of its diversified approach. It was not apparent during the Carter administration which of the technologies under development would prove useful in practice, nor is it obvious that different organization or significantly increased investment would have resulted in substantively improved outcomes for such programs as Assault Breaker. On the whole, it is not clear to what extent the offset strategy is useful as a model for present-day attempts to exploit emerging technologies for strategic advantage as some of its latter-day admirers suggest.

In summary, the insights gleaned from this case study that potentially align with our dimensions of posture assessment are as follows:

- **Organization, Advancement:** The development of single-component versus joint technologies presents different risks because of the level of coordination required and service owner-

---

[48] U.S. General Accounting Office, *Report to Congressional Committees: Tactical Intelligence: Joint STARS Full-Rate Production Decision Was Premature and Risky*, Washington, D.C., GAO/NSIAD-97-68, April 25, 1997.

[49] Keefer, 2017, pp. 588–589.

[50] In addition to the precision-guided antiarmor munitions envisioned by Assault Breaker, another associated capability—the BETA project for automated intelligence fusion—also exceeded the technology of the early 1980s.

ship. Striking a balance between both might therefore serve as an effective risk-mitigation strategy.

- **Advancement, Adoption:** The development of CONOPs and technologies should ideally take place concurrently with R&D. They should also be subjected to regular red-teaming, including for scenarios other than those of primary and immediate interest.

- **Organization, Advancement:** Finally, as we saw in the earlier case study on the history of AI in DoD and now reinforced in this case study, it might not generally be possible to identify which of the apparent opportunities are illusory, except by trial and error.

Adoption and Scaling of Unmanned Aircraft Systems

Although the background research carried out for this case study was broad,[51] covering the history of UAS in DoD dating back to the early 19th century, we emphasize in our summary here the part most relevant to our posture assessment, specifically the adoption and scaling of UAS into DoD after the terrorist attacks of September 11, 2001 (9/11), and the insights therein.

Prior to 9/11, spending on UAS programs within and outside the Air Force was greater during the Vietnam War than it had been at any other point between 1954 and 2000.[52] Despite strong advocacy from some Air Force leadership, challenges in identifying useful applications for UAS contributed to the failure of several UAS development efforts during that time. Likewise, in the 1970s and the 1980s, there were a plethora of UAS programs, but many of them were canceled because of lack of investment or persistent test failures. In the 1990s, the United States became more skilled with UAS in combat situations, particularly with the Pioneer, Hunter, Pointer, Exdrone, and Predator UAS, which

---

[51] The research for this case study drew upon 25 sources from the literature. Of those, we only reference here those sources that support the narrative leading up to the relevant insights.

[52] U.S. Air Force, *The U.S. Air Force Remotely Piloted Aircraft and Unmanned Aerial Vehicle Strategic Vision*, Washington, D.C., 2005.

proved useful in counterterrorism operations in Afghanistan, Iraq, and Syria. This use of UAS provided an important inflection point in UAS history, especially when UAS were equipped with a weapon, in combination with sensors.

After 9/11, the U.S. military Operation Enduring Freedom in Afghanistan (2001) and Operation Iraqi Freedom in Iraq (2003) used UAS not only for surveillance but, for the first time, for killing enemies. The medium-altitude MQ-1 Predator, and later the MQ-9 Reaper, were equipped with full-motion video and other types of sensors for ISR, but were also equipped with weapons for conducting strikes. Hence, they were capable of conducting both ISR and strike missions.

Spurred by then–Air Force Chief of Staff Ronald Fogleman to fully embrace UAS, DoD recognition of UAS warfighting capabilities led to a surge in development, acquisition, and deployment.[53] This recognition led to an explosion of available products from industry, which spread throughout the military services; between 2002 and 2011, the U.S. inventory of UAS of various types, sizes, and capabilities increased from just 167 to more than 7,000. As of 2013, the rate of UAS growth in DoD showed no signs of declining.

The ISR Task Force was established in April 2008, based on then–Secretary of Defense Gates' vision for the force, which focused on unconventional warfare.[54] The ISR Task Force, a temporary congressionally mandated task force, ultimately recommended that DoD "maximize the availability of systems in the inventory and . . . acquire adequate numbers of additional systems."[55] By March 2012, funding was obtained for Predator and Reaper-class orbits for 65 continuous

---

[53] Keric D. Clanahan, "Wielding a Very Long, People-Intensive Spear: Inherently Governmental Functions and the Role of Contractors in U.S. Department of Defense Unmanned Aircraft Systems Missions," *Air Force Law Review*, Vol. 70, December 22, 2013; Raphael S. Cohen, *Air Force Strategic Planning: Past, Present, and Future*, Santa Monica, Calif.: RAND Corporation, RR-1765-AF, 2017.

[54] Marshall Curtis Erwin, *Intelligence, Surveillance, and Reconnaissance (ISR) Acquisition: Issues for Congress*, Congressional Research Service: Washington, D.C., R41284, April 16, 2013.

[55] Erwin, 2013.

combat air patrols with the potential to increase to 85. By 2013, the ISR Task Force had spent $12 billion since its inception to expedite development and delivery of ISR technologies to Iraq and Afghanistan, many (but not all) of them UAS-related. The ISR Task Force was subsequently transitioned from the OSD to USD(I). The change was meant to ensure that urgent requirements for quick reaction capabilities would become more globally focused in the post-Afghanistan future.[56] The ISR Task Force was disbanded, and some of the roles and responsibilities of the task force transitioned to the USDI Director for Warfighter Support.[57]

In summary, the following insight gleaned from this case study potentially aligns with our dimensions of posture assessment:

- **Organization, Advancement, Adoption:** The identification of clear and measurable goals (in addition to the nonnegligible wartime pressures) would likely have aided the ISR Task Force to rapidly scale UAS from 33 to 65 combat air patrol.

Big Safari

Our last case study considered Big Safari, an agile acquisition organization within the Air Force, as an example of a program and organization that enables rapid capability development and flexibility for military intelligence (specifically, reconnaissance) through emphasis on modifications of existing vehicles and platforms.[58] For decades, DoD has contended with how to rapidly deliver intelligence (and other) capabilities urgently needed by warfighters in the face of slow acquisition systems, particularly as military intelligence needs can be dynamic and change

---

[56] Kris Osborn, "ISR Task Force's Murky Future Gets Clearer," *Military.com*, October 13, 2013.

[57] Janet A. McDonnell, "The Office of the Under Secretary of Defense for Intelligence: The First 10 Years," *Studies in Intelligence*, Vol. 58, No. 1, March 2014.

[58] The research for this case study drew upon five sources from the literature and personal communication. Of those, we only reference here those sources that support the narrative leading up to the relevant insights.

quickly in response to the warfighting environment. Military intelligence, like AI, has an intense reliance on data, rendering it an interesting case study from that perspective.

Big Safari—designated within the Air Force as the 645th Aeronautical Systems Group within AFMC—is headquartered at Ohio's Wright-Patterson Air Force Base. It is an agile acquisition organization for ISR set up in 1952. For many years, its existence was kept out of the public eye because of its dealings with special reconnaissance. Today, Big Safari receives guidance, requirements, and funding from both the Headquarters Air Force Intelligence Directorate and the SAF/AQ. It conducts rapid acquisition and sustainment of specialized capabilities of limited program scope (below a certain size in number of units or dollars) including or related to airborne ISR. One way to conceptualize Big Safari is as a rough equivalent to a program office for major capabilities, such as the F-35 Joint Strike Fighter, except that it manages many very small (in aircraft numbers) programs. Once the total number of aircraft in a Big Safari program exceeds several dozen (which rarely happens—though it did in the case of Predator), that program is moved to its own office and is managed more directly by the service.

Big Safari has a history of agile capability development relative to the mainstream acquisition, which has much longer turnaround times for requirements, competition, and development processes. As a result, it is able to respond to emerging needs within months to a year or two, as opposed to years or decades. Although the foundational legal guidelines must be followed in any case, Big Safari generally makes up time by working on niche capabilities, streamlining the process for defining requirements (generally easier with niche capabilities that are very focused on what gaps they are intended to fill), modifying existing capabilities, keeping programs small, and working extensively with selected partners.[59]

In sum, Big Safari presents an interesting and successful instantiation of a centralized management approach for rapid acquisition of

---

[59] Bill Grimes, *The History of Big Safari*, Bloomington, Ind.: Archway Publishing, 2014.

technologies. The secrets to its success in rapidly delivering capabilities that meet warfighting needs are threefold:

- **Organization:** It maintains a lean, well-defined mission that enables the organization to operate efficiently and with focus.
- **Organization, Adoption:** It serves as an enabling clearinghouse for matching warfighter needs with contractors (and funding) that can provide the capabilities.
- **Advancement, Adoption:** It focuses on modifications to existing aircraft and sensors, rather than starting new acquisition programs.

Defining Artificial Intelligence

In this appendix, we present the variety of definitions of AI encountered throughout the project. First, we present the definitions—or conceptualizations—of AI as articulated by our interviewees. Then we present the definitions adopted by relevant government agencies and policies.

Interviewee Input

We wanted to understand how our interviewees conceptualize the term AI, and whether they equate AI with ML, particularly because of the use of the term "AI/ML" in some circles. Having this information would help us compare, contrast, and synthesize the various points of view. We therefore tried in 75 of our interviews to touch upon what AI means.[1] Although we do not provide a definition of AI in this report, we highlight the disparate views on defining AI and the difficulties of settling on a meaningful definition, based on both our interviews and a review of existing definitions.

The variety of opinions we heard was very broad: Some interviewees defined AI in terms of technical approaches and others did so

---

[1] Of these 75 interviews, 46 were DoD interviews, nine were other government interviews, six were academic interviews, and 14 were industry interviews. Although we would have liked to address this question in all 102 interviews conducted, we sometimes opted to drop it if there were more-pressing questions that we needed to prioritize, given the limited interview time.

in terms of aspirational goals. A few interviewees defined AI in terms of specific capabilities or a specific set of problems to solve, and several interviewees commented that they avoid the use of the term AI. Two interviewees expressed the belief that the current interest in AI is really interest in ML, and nine interviewees strongly emphasized that AI is more than just ML. Several interviewees were keen on highlighting that AI does not aim to replace humans, but rather to augment their efforts. The diversity of opinions offered is not surprising, as the debate on how to define AI has been ongoing for decades. For comparison, in the next section, we describe some of the publicly available ("official") definitions of AI we identified, and we noted a similar lack of convergence.

We also asked 21 interviewees from the four groups (DoD, non-DoD, industry, and academia) whether they thought DoD would benefit from a unified DoD-wide definition of AI. Six answered no, 11 answered yes, and the remaining four had mixed feelings about the utility of such an endeavor. Some advocates argued that a unified definition would facilitate the creation of a common framework for defining objectives, establishing metrics to gauge success, and developing doctrine, and would help DoD stay in sync with academia and industry.[2] Other advocates thought that having a DoD-wide definition would help to get a handle on investments and talent, might help educate senior leaders and manage their expectations, and would create a common taxonomy of terms. One interviewee noted that having a common definition allowed their organization to put all their efforts under one umbrella and speak with a unified voice as an organization. Concerns regarding the establishment of a unified DoD-wide definition of AI included views that AI should be considered in terms of capabilities and that, as a result, the definition of AI will differ as a function of use, users, and specific technologies. Other concerns revolved around the inherent difficulties in establishing neat boundaries for AI, especially as they are constantly shifting. Several interviewees noted

---

[2] We note that last view was purely on the DoD side. Our non-DoD interviewees did not express a similar belief in response to the same question: "Would DoD benefit from a DoD-wide definition of AI?"

that a standardized definition would not prevent variability in downstream interpretation and application by the services and end-users. This can be interpreted both positively and negatively: If a definition is open for interpretation, it does not unnecessarily constrain stakeholders. By the same token, it might not solve the practical problem of how to delineate AI investments or AI talent in DoD.

Existing Definitions

For ease of reference, we collect in this section some definitions of AI put forth by federal, academic, and technical sources. A recent Congressional Research Service report sums it up nicely by noting that "[a]lmost all academic studies in artificial intelligence acknowledge that no commonly accepted definition of AI exists, in part because of the diverse approaches to research in the field."[3]

FY 2019 National Defense Authorization Act

The FY19 NDAA provides the following definition for AI in Section 238(g):

(1) Any artificial system that performs tasks under varying and unpredictable circumstances without significant human oversight, or that can learn from experience and improve performance when exposed to data sets.

(2) An artificial system developed in computer software, physical hardware, or other context that solves tasks requiring human-like perception, cognition, planning, learning, communication, or physical action.

(3) An artificial system designed to think or act like a human, including cognitive architectures and neural networks.

---

[3] Kelley M. Sayler, *Artificial Intelligence and National Security*, Washington, D.C.: Congressional Research Service, R45178, January 30, 2019, p. 1.

(4) A set of techniques, including machine learning (ML), that is designed to approximate a cognitive task.

(5) An artificial system designed to act rationally, including an intelligent software agent or embodied robot that achieves goals using perception, planning, reasoning, learning, communicating, decision making, and acting.[4]

2018 DoD AI Strategy

The summary of the 2018 DoD AI strategy states that "AI refers to the ability of machines to perform tasks that normally require human intelligence—for example, recognizing patterns, learning from experience, drawing conclusions, making predictions, or taking action—whether digitally or as the smart software behind autonomous physical systems."[5]

DARPA

A former director of DARPA's Information Innovation Office (I2O) defined AI as the "programmed ability to process information," and highlighted three (successive) waves of AI demonstrating various levels of progress along four dimensions:[6] perception, learning, abstraction, and reasoning.[7]

National Science and Technology Council

A report by the NSTC states that "There is no single definition of AI that is universally accepted by practitioners. Some define AI loosely as a computerized system that exhibits behavior that is commonly thought

---

[4] Pub. L. 115–232, 2018.

[5] U.S. Department of Defense, 2018d, p. 5.

[6] The three waves of AI are (1) handcrafted knowledge, in reference to the expert systems favored through the 1980s, (2) statistical learning, in reference to the ML approaches, including neural network models, developed in the 1980s and demonstrating their potential today and (3) contextual adaptation, anticipated to constitute the next evolution of AI (John Launchbury, "A DARPA Perspective on Artificial Intelligence," video, YouTube, 2017).

[7] Launchbury, 2017.

of as requiring intelligence. Others define AI as a system capable of rationally solving complex problems or taking appropriate actions to achieve its goals in whatever real world circumstances it encounters."[8]

National Science Foundation

Peter Atherton of America's Seed Fund, which is powered by the NSF, writes the following on the fund's webpage about AI: "This topic focuses on innovations in the field of artificial intelligence (AI), which refers to intelligence exhibited by machines or software. AI is not a specific technology or technical method—it is instead a field of study aimed at achieving machine-based intelligence. Current AI technologies are targeted at specific problem sets. Artificial general intelligence—machines that can reason like humans—remains a more elusive long-term goal."[9]

A 2019 NSF National AI Research Institutes request for proposals says the following about the definition of AI:

> AI enables computers and other automated systems to perform tasks that have historically required human cognition and human decision-making abilities. Research in AI is therefore concerned with the understanding of the mechanisms underlying thought and intelligent behavior and their implementation in machines. The full AI endeavor is inherently multidisciplinary, encompassing the research necessary to understand and develop systems that can perceive, learn, reason, communicate, and act in the world; exhibit flexibility, resourcefulness, creativity, real-time responsiveness, and long-term reflection; use a variety of representation or reasoning approaches; and demonstrate competence in complex environments and social contexts.[10]

---

[8] National Science and Technology Council and Office of Science and Technology Policy, 2016b, p. 6.

[9] Peter Atherton, "Technology Topic: Artificial Intelligence (AI)," America's Seed Fund, webpage, undated.

[10] National Science Foundation, "Program Solicitation NSF 20-503: National Artificial Intelligence (AI) Research Institutes: Accelerating Research, Transforming Society, and Growing the American Workforce," request for proposals, 2019.

National Institute of Standards and Technology

A 2019 NIST report cited definitions of AI that have been put forth by the American National Standards Institute:[11]

> (1) A branch of computer science devoted to developing data processing systems that performs functions normally associated with human intelligence, such as reasoning, learning, and self-improvement. (2) The capability of a device to perform functions that are normally associated with human intelligence such as reasoning, learning, and self-improvement.

The NIST report also cites a definition from the International Organization for Standardization and the International Electrotechnical Commission:

> **artificial intelligence:** capability of a system to acquire, process, and apply knowledge

> **Note 1 to entry:** knowledge are facts, information, and skills acquired through experience or education

> **AI system:** technical system that uses artificial intelligence to solve problems.[12]

American Association for Artificial Intelligence

The American Association for Artificial Intelligence (AAAI)[13] states on its website that it aims to advance the scientific understanding of

---

[11] National Institute of Standards and Technology, 2019, p. 25.

[12] National Institute of Standards and Technology, 2019, p. 25.

[13] The AAAI is an international nonprofit scientific society established in 1979. It sponsors multiple conferences and symposia, including the AAAI Conference on Artificial Intelligence, considered one of the leading conferences in the field; supports 14 journals; and publishes the quarterly *AI Magazine*.

"the mechanisms underlying thought and intelligent behavior and their embodiment in machines."[14]

Government Accountability Office

Although the Government Accountability Office does not explicitly define artificial intelligence in its recent technology assessment report on AI, it introduces the field in this manner while noting that AI has been defined in a variety of ways:

> "The field of AI was founded on the idea that machines could be used to simulate human intelligence. AI has been defined in a variety of ways, and researchers have also distinguished between narrow and general AI. Narrow AI refers to applications that provide domain-specific expertise or task completion, including today's robotics and applications such as tax preparation software and on-line "chatbots," which answer questions specific to a product or service. General AI refers to an AI system that exhibits intelligence comparable to that of a human, or beyond, across the variety of contexts in which a human might interact. Fictional examples of general AI include the computer H.A.L., from the film *2001: A Space Odyssey*, and Lieutenant Commander Data, from the *Star Trek: The Next Generation* television series."[15]

---

[14] Association for the Advancement of Artificial Intelligence, "The AAAI Conference on Artificial Intelligence," webpage, undated.

[15] U.S. Government Accountability Office, *Artificial Intelligence: Emerging Opportunities, Challenges, and Implications: Highlights of a Forum Convened by the Comptroller General of the United States*, Washington, D.C., GAO-18-142SP, March 2018.

References

Air Force Institute of Technology, "AFIT Civilian Institution Programs," webpage, undated. As of November 14, 2019:
https://cip.afit.edu/cip/

Åkersten, Ingvar, "The Strategic Computing Program," in Allan M. Din, ed., *Arms and Artificial Intelligence: Weapon and Arms Control Applications of Advanced Computing*, New York: Oxford University Press, 1987, pp. 87–99.

Albliwi, Saja A., Jiju Antony, and Norin Arshed, "Critical Literature Review on Maturity Models for Business Process Excellence," *2014 IEEE International Conference on Industrial Engineering and Engineering Management*, 2015, pp. 79–83.

AlphaStar Team, "AlphaStar: Mastering the Real-Time Strategy Game StarCraft II," webpage, 2019. As of October 21, 2019:
https://deepmind.com/blog/article/
alphastar-mastering-real-time-strategy-game-starcraft-ii

Anton, Philip S., Megan McKernan, Ken Munson, James G. Kallimani, Alexis Levedahl, Irv Blickstein, Jeffrey A. Drezner, and Sydne Newberry, *Assessing the Use of Data Analytics in Department of Defense Acquisition*, Santa Monica, Calif.: RAND Corporation, RB-10085-OSD, 2019. As of October 21, 2019:
https://www.rand.org/pubs/research_briefs/RB10085.html

Army Science Board, *Robotic and Autonomous Systems of Systems Architecture*, Department of the Army, January 15, 2017.

Association for Computing Machinery, "'The Power and Limits of Machine Learning' with Yann LeCun," video, YouTube, September 11, 2019. As of October 23, 2019:
https://www.youtube.com/watch?v=zikdDOzOpxY

Association for the Advancement of Artificial Intelligence, "The AAAI Conference on Artificial Intelligence," webpage, undated. As of October 21, 2019:
http://aaai.org/

Atherton, Peter, "Technology Topic: Artificial Intelligence (AI)," America's Seed Fund, webpage, undated. As of October 21, 2019: https://seedfund.nsf.gov/topics/artificial-intelligence/

Automatic Language Processing Advisory Committee, *Language and Machines: Computers in Translation and Linguistics*, Washington, D.C.: National Academy of Sciences, National Research Council, Publication 1416, 1966.

Barrett, Brian, "McDonald's Doubles Down on Tech with Voice AI Acquisition," *Wired*, September 10, 2019.

Baxter, Pamela, and Susan Jack, "Qualitative Case Study Methodology: Study Design and Implementation for Novice Researchers," *Qualitative Report,* Vol. 13, No. 4, December 1, 2008.

Bishop, Christopher M., *Pattern Recognition and Machine Learning (Information Science and Statistics)*, 2nd edition, New York: Springer, 2011.

Bryson, John M., Lauren Hamilton Edwards, and David M. Van Slyke, "Getting Strategic About Strategic Planning Research," *Public Management Review,* Vol. 20, No. 3, 2018, pp. 317–339.

Chief of Naval Operations, U.S. Navy, *A Design for Maintaining Maritime Superiority*, version 2.0, Washington, D.C., December 2018.

Chu, David S. C., testimony before the National Commission on Military, National, and Public Service, Washington, D.C., May 16, 2019.

Clanahan, Keric D., "Wielding a Very Long, People-Intensive Spear: Inherently Governmental Functions and the Role of Contractors in U.S. Department of Defense Unmanned Aircraft Systems Missions," *Air Force Law Review*, Vol. 70, December 22, 2013, pp. 119–204.

Cohen, Raphael S., *Air Force Strategic Planning: Past, Present, and Future*, Santa Monica, Calif.: RAND Corporation, RR-1765-AF, 2017. As of October 21, 2019: https://www.rand.org/pubs/research_reports/RR1765.html

Crevier, Daniel, *AI: The Tumultuous History of the Search for Artificial Intelligence*, New York: Basic Books, 1993.

Deasy, Dana, statement before the Senate Armed Services Committee Subcommittee on Cyber Security, "On DoD Cybersecurity Policies and Architecture," Washington, D.C.: U.S. Senate, 2019.

Defense Acquisition University, "Digital Acquisition Prototypes," webpage, undated. As of October 28, 2019: https://aaf.dau.edu

Defense Advanced Research Projects Agency, *DARPA: Defense Advanced Research Projects Agency: 1958-2018*, Tampa, Fla.: Faircount Media Group, 2018.

Defense Innovation Board, *AI Principles: Recommendations on the Ethical Use of Artificial Intelligence by the Department of Defense*, undated a.

———, "Our Work: Recommendations," webpage, undated b. As of October 21, 2019:
https://innovation.defense.gov/Recommendations/

———, *Software Is Never Done: Refactoring the Acquisition Code for Competitive Advantage*, Washington, D.C., March 12, 2019a.

———, *SWAP Main Report*, Washington, D.C., May 3, 2019b.

Department of Defense Directive 1200.17, *Managing the Reserve Components as an Operational Force*, Washington, D.C., October 29, 2008.

Department of Defense Instruction 5000.02, *Operation of Defense Acquisition System*, Washington, D.C., January 7, 2015.

Department of Defense Instruction 1400.25, *DoD Civilian Personnel Management System: Employment of Highly Qualified Experts (HQEs)*, Washington, D.C., incorporating Change 1, January 18, 2017.

Department of Defense Standard 1679A, *Military Standard Software Development*, Washington, D.C., DOD-STD-1679, Revision A, October 22, 1983.

Department of Defense Standard 2167A, *Defense System Software Development*, Washington, D.C., DOD-STD-2167A, February 29, 1988.

Deputy Secretary of Defense, "Establishment of the Joint Artificial Intelligence Center," memorandum to military staff, Washington, D.C.: U.S. Department of Defense, June 27, 2018.

Drezner, Jeffrey A., Megan McKernan, Austin Lewis, Ken Munson, Devon Hill, Jaime L. Hastings, Geoffrey McGovern, Marek N. Posard, and Jerry M. Sollinger, *Issues with Access to Acquisition Data and Information in the Department of Defense: Identification and Characterization of Data for Acquisition Category (ACAT) II–IV, Pre-MDAPs, and Defense Business Systems*, Santa Monica, Calif.: RAND Corporation, March 2019, Not available to the general public.

Druffel, Larry, *A Technical History of the SEI*, Pittsburgh, Pa.: Carnegie Mellon University, CMU/SEI-2016-SR-027, January 2017.

Erwin, Marshall Curtis, *Intelligence, Surveillance, and Reconnaissance (ISR) Acquisition: Issues for Congress*, Congressional Research Service: Washington, D.C., R41284, April 16, 2013.

Executive Office of the President, *Charter of the National Science and Technology Council Select Committee on Artificial Intelligence*, Washington, D.C., 2018.

Fountaine, Tim, Brian McCarthy, and Tamim Saleh, "Building the AI-Powered Organization," *Harvard Business Review*, July–August 2019.

Fryer-Biggs, Zachary, "Inside the Pentagon's Plan to Win Over Silicon Valley's AI Experts," *Wired*, December 21, 2018.

Gates, Robert M., *Duty: Memoirs of a Secretary at War*, New York: Vintage Books, 2014.

Gill, Roger, "Change Management—Or Change Leadership?" *Journal of Change Management*, Vol. 3, No. 4, 2002, pp. 307–318.

Gofman, Michael, and Zhao Jin, "Artificial Intelligence, Human Capital, and Innovation," University of Rochester, working paper, August 20, 2019.

Gomes, Lee, "Facebook AI Director Yann LeCun on His Quest to Unleash Deep Learning and Make Machines Smarter," *IEEE Spectrum*, February 18, 2015.

Grimes, Bill, *The History of Big Safari*, Bloomington, Ind.: Archway Publishing, 2014.

Harkins, Gina, "Marine Commandant: You Can Have Purple Hair in Our New Cyber Force," *Military.com*, April 29, 2019.

Hastie, Trevor, Robert Tibshirani, and Jerome Friedman, *The Elements of Statistical Learning: Data Mining, Inference, and Prediction*, 2nd ed., New York: Springer, 2009, corrected at 12th printing, 2017.

ImageNet, homepage, undated. As of October 28, 2019:
https://www.image-net.org

Joint Chiefs of Staff, *The National Military Strategy of the United States of America: A Strategy for Today, a Vision for Tomorrow*, Washington, D.C.: U.S. Department of Defense, 2004.

———, *Charter of the Joint Requirements Oversight Council (JROC) and Implementation of the Joint Capabilities Integration and Development System (JCIDS)*, Washington, D.C., CJCSI 5123.01H, August 31, 2018.

Keefer, Edward C., *Harold Brown: Offsetting the Soviet Military Challenge, 1977–1981*, Washington, D.C.: Historical Office, Office of the Secretary of Defense, 2017.

Khetarpal, Khimya, Zafarali Ahmed, Andre Cianflone, Riashat Islam, and Joelle Pineau, "RE-EVALUATE: Reproducibility in Evaluating Reinforcement Learning Algorithms," paper presented at the International Conference on Machine Learning, Stockholm, Sweden, 2018.

Knight, Will, "An AI Pioneer Wants His Algorithms to Understand the 'Why,'" *Wired*, October 8, 2019.

Knopp, Bradley M., Sina Beaghley, Aaron Frank, Rebeca Orrie, and Michael Watson, *Defining the Roles, Responsibilities, and Functions for Data Science Within the Defense Intelligence Agency*, Santa Monica, Calif.: RAND Corporation, RR-1582-DIA, 2016. As of October 21, 2019:
https://www.rand.org/pubs/research_reports/RR1582.html

Kotter, John P., "Leading Change: Why Transformation Effort Fails," *Harvard Business Review*, May–June 1995.

Krizan, Lisa, "Intelligence Essentials for Everyone," Occasional Paper, No. 6, Washington, D.C.: Joint Military Intelligence College, June 1999.

Krizhevsky, Alex, Ilya Sutskever, and Geoffrey E. Hinton, "ImageNet Classification with Deep Convolutional Neural Networks," *Communications of the ACM*, Vol. 60, No. 6, June 2017, pp. 84–90.

Larman, Craig, and Victor R. Basili, "Iterative and Incremental Development: A Brief History," *Computer*, Vol. 36, No. 6, June 2003, pp. 2–11.

Launchbury, John, "A DARPA Perspective on Artificial Intelligence," video, YouTube, 2017. As of October 21, 2019:
https://www.youtube.com/watch?v=-O01G3tSYpU

LeCun, Yann, Yoshua Bengio, and Geoffrey Hinton, "Deep Learning," *Nature,* Vol. 521, May 28, 2015, pp. 436–444.

"Manifesto for Agile Software Development," webpage, undated. As of October 29, 2019:
http://agilemanifesto.org

Matheson, Rob, "MIT and U.S. Air Force Sign Agreement to Launch AI Accelerator," *MIT News*, blog post, May 20, 2019. As of November 1, 2019:
http://news.mit.edu/2019/
mit-and-us-air-force-sign-agreement-new-ai-accelerator-0520

Matt, Christian, Thomas Hess, and Alexander Benlian, "Digital Transformation Strategies," *Business and Information Systems Engineering*, Vol. 57, No. 5, 2015, pp. 339-343.

McDonnell, Janet A., "The Office of the Under Secretary of Defense for Intelligence: The First 10 Years," *Studies in Intelligence,* Vol. 58, No. 1, March 2014, pp. 9–16.

Mikolov, Tomas, Kai Chen, Greg Corrado, and Jeffrey Dean, "Efficient Estimation of Word Representations in Vector Space," *arXiv:1301.3781,* September 7, 2013.

Miller, Ron, "S&P Global Snares Kensho for $550 Million," *TechCrunch*, March 7, 2018.

Nagel, Matthew, "Army AI Task Force Selects Carnegie Mellon as New Hub," Carnegie Mellon University, blog post, December 4, 2018. As of October 24, 2019:
https://www.cmu.edu/news/stories/archives/2018/december/
army-ai-task-force.html

National Defense Industrial Association, "DoD Rewrite of 5000 Series to Include a Software Acquisition Pathway," webpage, July 26, 2019. As of October 21, 2019:
https://www.ndia.org/policy/recent-posts/2019/7/26/
dod-rewrite-of-5000-series-to-include-a-software-acquisition-pathway

National Institute of Standards and Technology, *U.S. Leadership in AI: A Plan for Federal Engagement in Developing Technical Standards and Related Tools*, U.S. Department of Commerce, August 9, 2019.

National Research Council, *Funding a Revolution: Government Support for Computing Research*, Washington, D.C.: National Academy Press, 1999.

National Science and Technology Council and Office of Science and Technology Policy, *The National Artificial Intelligence Research and Development Strategic Plan*, Washington, D.C.: Executive Office of the President, October 2016a.

———, *Preparing for the Future of Artificial Intelligence*, Washington, D.C.: Executive Office of the President, October 2016b.

National Science Foundation, "Program Solicitation NSF 20-503: National Artificial Intelligence (AI) Research Institutes: Accelerating Research, Transforming Society, and Growing the American Workforce," request for proposals, 2019.

National Security Commission on Artificial Intelligence, *Initial Report*, Washington, D.C., July 31, 2019a.

———, *Interim Report*, Washington, D.C., November 2019b.

Neema, Sandeep, "Assured Autonomy," Defense Advanced Research Projects Agency, webpage, undated. As of October 24, 2019:
https://www.darpa.mil/program/assured-autonomy

Newhouse, William, Stephanie Keith, Benjamin Scribner, and Greg Witter, *National Initiative for Cybersecurity Education (NICE) Cybersecurity Workforce Framework*, Gaithersburg, Md.: National Institute of Standards and Technology, U.S. Department of Commerce, NIST Special Publication 800–181, August 2017.

Obama, Barack, *International Strategy for Cyberspace: Prosperity, Security, and Openness in a Networked World*, White House: Washington, D.C., May 2011.

Office of the Director of National Intelligence, *The AIM Initiative: A Strategy for Augmenting Intelligence Using Machines*, Washington, D.C., January 16, 2019.

Orazem, Geoff, Greg Mallory, Matthew Schlueter, and Danny Werfel, "Why Startups Don't Bid on Government Contracts," Boston Consulting Group, webpage, August 22, 2017. As of October 21, 2017:
https://www.bcg.com/en-us/publications/2017/public-sector-agency-transformation-why-startups-dont-bid-government-contracts.aspx

Osborn, Kris, "ISR Task Force's Murky Future Gets Clearer," *Military.com*, October 13, 2013. As of November 14, 2019:
https://www.military.com/daily-news/2013/10/19/isr-task-forces-murky-future-gets-clearer.html

Partnership on AI, "About ML: Annotation and Benchmarking on Understanding and Transparency of Machine Learning Lifecycles," webpage, undated. As of October 29, 2019:
https://partnershiponai.org/about-ml/

Perry, William J., "Desert Storm and Deterrence," *Foreign Affairs*, Vol. 70, No. 4, Fall 1991.

Porche, Isaac R., III, Shawn McKay, Megan McKernan, Robert Warren Button, Bob Murphy, Katheryn Giglio, and Elliot Axelband, *Rapid Acquisition and Fielding for Information Assurance and Cyber Security in the Navy*, Santa Monica, Calif.: RAND Corporation, TR-1294-NAVY, 2012. As of October 21, 2019:
https://www.rand.org/pubs/technical_reports/TR1294.html

Porter, Lisa, statement to the House Armed Services Committee and Subcommittee on Emerging Threats and Capabilities, "Department of Defense's Artificial Intelligence Structures, Investments, and Applications," Washington, D.C., U.S. House of Representatives, December 11, 2018.

Public Law 91–121, An Act to Authorize Appropriations During the Fiscal Year 1970, Title II, Section 203, November 19, 1969.

Public Law 114–113, Consolidated Appropriations Act, 2016, Title III, Federal Cybersecurity Workforce Assessment Act of 2015, December 18, 2015.

Public Law 115–232, John S. McCain National Defense Authorization Act for Fiscal Year 2019, August 13, 2018.

Ripple, Bryan, "Skyborg Program Seeks Industry Input for Artificial Intelligence Initiative," U.S. Air Force, webpage, March 27, 2019. As of October 23, 2019:
https://www.af.mil/News/Article-Display/Article/1796930/skyborg-program-seeks-industry-input-for-artificial-intelligence-initiative/

Russakovsky, Olga, Jia Deng, Hao Su, Jonathan Krause, Sanjeev Satheesh, Sean Ma, Zhiheng Huang, Andrej Karpathy, Aditya Khosla, Michael Bernstein, Alexander C. Berg, and Li Fei-Fei, "ImageNet Large Scale Visual Recognition Challenge," *International Journal of Computer Vision*, Vol. 115, No. 3, December 2015, pp. 211–252.

Sayler, Kelley M., *Artificial Intelligence and National Security*, Washington, D.C.: Congressional Research Service, R45178, January 30, 2019.

Secretary of the Navy, *Cybersecurity Readiness Review*, Washington, D.C.: Department of the Navy, March 4, 2019.

Section 809 Panel, *Report of the Advisory Panel on Streamlining and Codifying Acquisition Regulations*, Vol. 2, June 2018.

Select Committee on Artificial Intelligence of the National Science and Technology Council, *The National Artificial Intelligence Research and Development Strategic Plan: 2019 Update*, Washington, D.C.: Executive Office of the President, June 2019.

Shanahan, John, "Artificial Intelligence Initiatives," statement to the Senate Armed Services Committee Subcommittee on Emerging Threats and Capabilities, Washington, D.C.: U.S. Senate, March 12, 2019.

Siegelmann, Hava, "Lifelong Learning Machines (L2M)," Defense Advanced Research Projects Agency, webpage, undated. As of October 24, 2019: https://www.darpa.mil/program/lifelong-learning-machines

Silver, David, Thomas Hubert, Julian Schrittwieser, Ioannis Antonoglou, Matthew Lai, Arthur Guez, Marc Lanctot, Laurent Sifre, Dharshan Kumaran, Thore Graepel, Timothy Lillicrap, Kern Simonyan, and Demis Hassabis, "Mastering Chess and Shogi By Self-Play with a General Reinforcement Learning Algorithm," *arXiv: 1712.01815*, 2017.

Silver, David, Julian Schrittwieser, Karen Simonyan, Ioannis Antonoglou, Aja Huang, Arthur Guez, Thomas Hubert, Lucas Baker, Matthew Lai, Adrian Bolton, Yutian Chen, Timothy Lillicrap, Fan Hui, Laurent Sifre, George van den Driessche, Thore Graepel, and Demis Hassabis, "Mastering the Game of Go Without Human Knowledge," *Nature*, Vol. 550, October 19, 2017, pp. 354–359.

Software Engineering Institute, "Brief History of CMMI," Carnegie Mellon University, 2009.

Szegedy, Christian, Wojciech Zaremba, Ilya Sutskever, Joan Bruna, Dumitru Erhan, Ian Goodfellow, and Rob Fergus, "Intriguing Properties of Neural Networks," *arXiv: 1312.6199*, December 21, 2013.

Tadjdeh, Yasmin, "AI Project to Link Military, Silicon Valley," *National Defense*, February 7, 2019.

"The Race for AI: Here Are the Tech Giants Rushing to Snap Up Artificial Intelligence Startups," CBInsights, webpage, September 17, 2019. As of October 29, 2019: http://cbinsights.com/research/top-acquirers-ai-startups-ma-timeline

Trump, Donald J., *Executive Order on Maintaining American Leadership in Artificial Intelligence*, Washington, D.C.: The White House, February 11, 2019.

Under Secretary of the Army, "Army Artificial Intelligence Strategy Annex Submission," memorandum for Chief Information Office, Office of the Secretary of Defense, Washington, D.C.: U.S. Department of Defense, 2019.

U.S. Air Force, *The U.S. Air Force Remotely Piloted Aircraft and Unmanned Aerial Vehicle Strategic Vision*, Washington, D.C., 2005.

U.S. Air Force Scientific Advisory Board, *Enhanced Utility of Unmanned Aerial Vehicles in Contested and Denied Environments*, Washington, D.C.: Department of the Air Force, 2015.

———, *Maintaining Technology Superiority for the United States Air Force (MTS)*, Washington, D.C.: Department of the Air Force, 2018.

U.S. Department of the Air Force, *The United States Air Force Artificial Intelligence Annex to the Department of Defense Artificial Intelligence Strategy*, Washington, D.C., 2019.

U.S. Department of Defense, *Software Acquisition Pathway Policy*, predecisional draft, Washington, D.C., undated, Not available to the general public.

———, "Fact Sheet: 2018 DoD Cyber Strategy and Cyber Posture Review," Washington, D.C., 2018a. As of October 29, 2019:
https://dodcio.defense.gov/Portals/0/Documents/Factsheet_for_Strategy_and_CPR_FINAL.pdf

———, *Nuclear Posture Review*, Washington, D.C., February 2018b.

———, *Summary of the 2018 Department of Defense Artificial Intelligence Strategy: Harnessing AI to Advance Our Security and Prosperity*, Washington, D.C., 2018c.

———, *Summary of the 2018 National Defense Strategy of the United States of America: Sharpening the American Military's Competitive Edge*, Washington, D.C., 2018d.

———, *Summary: Department of Defense Cyber Strategy*, Washington, DC, 2018e.

U.S. Department of Defense, Chief Management Officer, "Deputy's Management Action Group (DMAG)," webpage, undated. As of November 1, 2019:
https://cmo.defense.gov/Resources/Deputys-Management-Action-Group

U.S. Department of Defense, Office of Publication and Security Review, *DoD Digital Modernization Strategy: DoD Information Resource Management Strategic Plan FY19–23*, Washington, D.C., July 12, 2019.

U.S. Department of Defense and the Defense Science Board, *Task Force Report: The Role of Autonomy in DoD Systems*, Washington, D.C., July 2012.

U.S. Department of Energy, "Secretary Perry Stands Up Office for Artificial Intelligence and Technology," September 6, 2019.

U.S. General Accounting Office, *Report to Congressional Committees: Tactical Intelligence: Joint STARS Full-Rate Production Decision Was Premature and Risky*, Washington, D.C., GAO/NSIAD-97-68, April 25, 1997.

U.S. Government Accountability Office, *Artificial Intelligence: Emerging Opportunities, Challenges, and Implications: Highlights of a Forum Convened by the Comptroller General of the United States*, Washington, D.C., GAO-18-142SP, March 2018.

U.S. Naval Research Advisory Committee, *Naval Research Advisory Committee Report: How Autonomy Can Transform Naval Operations*, Washington, D.C., Office of the Secretary of the Navy, October 2012.

———, *Autonomous and Unmanned Systems in the Department of the Navy*, September 2017.

Van Atta, Richard H., Alethia Cook, Ivars Gutmanis, Michael J. Lippitz, and Jasper Lupo, *Transformation and Transition: DARPA's Role in Fostering an Emerging Revolution in Military Affairs,* Vol. 2, *Detailed Assessments,* Alexandria, Va.: Institute for Defense Analyses, November 2003.

Waltz, M., and K. Fu, "A Heuristic Approach to Reinforcement Learning Control Systems," *IEEE Transactions on Automatic Control,* Vol. 10, No. 4, October 1965, pp. 390–398.

Werber, Laura, John A. Ausink, Lindsay Daugherty, Brian M. Phillips, Felix Knutson, and Ryan Haberman, *An Assessment of Gaps in Business Acumen and Knowledge of Industry Within the Defense Acquisition Workforce,* Santa Monica, Calif.: RAND Corporation, RR-2825-OSD, 2019. As of November 14, 2019: https://www.rand.org/pubs/research_reports/RR2825.html

Work, Bob, speech delivered at convocation exercises at National Defense University, Washington, D.C., August 5, 2014.

Yin, Robert K., *Case Study Research: Design and Methods,* 3rd ed., Thousand Oaks, Calif.: SAGE Publications, 2003.